T0389725

A Decade of Zimbabwe

A Decade of Zimbabwe

Politics, Economy and Society 2008–2017

By

Amin Kamete

BRILL

LEIDEN | BOSTON

Library of Congress Cataloging-in-Publication Data

Names: Kamete, Amin Y., author.
Title: A decade of Zimbabwe : politics, economy and society 2008–2017 / by
Amin Kamete.
Description: Leiden ; Boston : Brill, 2019. |
Identifiers: LCCN 2019015070 (print) | LCCN 2019015535 (ebook) |
ISBN 9789004404335 (E-book) | ISBN 9789004349063 (pbk. : alk. paper)
Subjects: LCSH: Zimbabwe—Politics and government—21st century. |
Zimbabwe—Economic conditions—21st century. | Zimbabwe—Social
conditions—21st century.
Classification: LCC DT2996 (ebook) | LCC DT2996 .K36 2019 (print) |
DDC 968.91051—dc23
LC record available at https://lccn.loc.gov/2019015070

Typeface for the Latin, Greek, and Cyrillic scripts: "Brill". See and download: brill.com/brill-typeface.

ISBN 978-90-04-34906-3 (paperback)
ISBN 978-90-04-40433-5 (e-book)

Contents

Zimbabwe in 2008

Landmark elections, a political stalemate, the resurgence of political violence, the absence of a proper government, SADC-mediated talks and a damaging cholera outbreak joined the deteriorating economy at the top of the domestic political and socioeconomic agenda. In foreign affairs, Zimbabwe's relations with the West remained frosty. Some voices from within Africa broke ranks with most of the continent and publicly condemned the ZANU-PF government.

Domestic Politics

In an extraordinary government gazette on 24 January, President Robert Mugabe announced that *presidential, general and local elections* would be held on 29 March. Parliament would be dissolved on 28 March. The announcement was criticised by the opposition Movement for Democratic Change (MDC) and civil society, and MDC would have preferred the elections to be held under a new constitution. The announcement was a setback to the interparty talks mediated by South African President Thabo Mbeki, whose apparent efforts to have the elections postponed failed. On 5 February, a former finance minister, *Simba Makoni*, who had defected from ZANU-PF, announced his candidacy for the presidency. There was widespread speculation that Makoni had the backing of the vice president, Joice Mujuru, and her husband, retired General Solomon Mujuru. On 12 January, Dumiso Dabengwa, a senior member of ZANU-PF and former cabinet minister, announced that he would support Makoni's presidential bid. Cyril Ndebele, the former speaker of parliament, also backed Makoni. While predicting that Makoni's candidacy would split the ZANU-PF vote, analysts also indicated that this would dilute the opposition vote. This was confirmed when the smaller MDC faction (MDC-Mutambara) publicly announced that it

 | DOI:10.1163/9789004404335_002

would back Makoni. The party would, however, separately contest the parliamentary, local government and senate elections.

On 10 January, the Zimbabwe Election Support Network (ZESN) already began to expose the *election problems* that would seriously compromise the results. In addition to violence, there were problems with voter education and registration. Despite some changes to the media and security laws and regulations in the run-up to the elections and as part of the interparty talks, President Mugabe and his ZANU-PF were accused of controlling all aspects of the electoral process. In particular, the registrar general, appointed by Mugabe, was accused of trying to rig the elections in ZANU-PF's favour by, among other things, manipulating the voters' roll. In February, President Mugabe launched his election campaign. In his rallies across the country he blamed the West, particularly the UK, for Zimbabwe's economic problems. He promised to end those problems when elected.

Election results changed the political landscape considerably. The opposition won control of parliament. Of the 206 contested seats, ZANU-PF won 96, MDC-Tsvangirai (MDC-T) 99, and MDC-M 10. One seat was won by Jonathan Moyo, the former information minister, who had contested as an independent candidate. In the senate elections, ZANU-PF garnered 30 seats, MDC-T 24, and MDC-M 6. Crucially, the opposition won seats in ZANU-PF's rural strongholds.

There were speculations that Morgan Tsvangirai had won the presidential poll. The MDC-T confirmed these by claiming that Tsvangirai had won 50.3% of the vote. Citing logistical problems and the need for a recount, the Zimbabwe Electoral Commission (ZEC) did not immediately release the presidential results, notwithstanding the fact that they were public knowledge thanks to the constitutional changes that stipulated that election results had to be displayed outside polling stations. The army relocated the vote-counting centre to a secret place and barred opposition and independent monitoring groups from witnessing the recount. Meanwhile, as the recount dragged on, there were allegations of *harassment, violence and intimidation* against the opposition and civil society. On 25 April, 250 policeman raided the MDC-T headquarters. ZESN offices were also raided. In the raid on the MDC-T headquarters some 300 people were arrested for allegedly engaging in post-election violence.

On 2 May, ZEC finally announced the results of the *presidential election.* Tsvangirai got 47.9%, Mugabe 43.7%, Makoni 8.3%, and independent candidate Langton Towungana 0.6%. MDC-T dismissed the result as "scandalous daylight robbery". Since none of the candidates had won an absolute majority, a *round run-off* was to be held within three weeks of the announcement of the results. However, ZEC controversially announced that the run-off would take place on 27 June. This was interpreted as a ploy by ZANU-PF to allow Mugabe to gain the advantage through violence or rigging. The results of the parliamentary elections were thrown into turmoil as the two biggest parties (ZANU-PF and MDC-T) challenged many of the results. ZANU-PF claimed the MDC-T had bribed ZEC officials to rig the election in its favour. At least 100 officials and polling officers were arrested.

Rumours were rife that Mugabe had lost the election and the tight *circle of securocrats* in the Joint Operations Command (JOC) had advised him not to concede defeat. The JOC was made up of Constantine Chiwenga, commander of the Zimbabwe Defence Forces (ZDF); Perence Shiri, commander of the air force of Zimbabwe; Augustine Chihuri, commissioner-general of the Zimbabwe Republic Police (ZRP); Paradzai Zimondi, head of the Zimbabwe prison services; Happyton Bonyongwe, director-general of the Central Intelligence Organisation (CIO); and Philip Sibanda, commander of the Zimbabwe National Army (ZNA). Emmerson Mnangagwa – back in Mugabe's favour after being sidelined since late 2004 – headed the JOC. Dubbed a 'military junta' by critics, the JOC was believed to be effectively running the country.

The period leading up to the presidential run-off was characterised by widespread *state violence* against and repression of suspected opposition supporters, especially in rural areas. Some 200 people were reportedly murdered, many were tortured and more than 200,000 displaced. Even after the election, violence continued. On 2 July, some 220 Zimbabweans sought refuge at the US embassy in Harare. Morgan Tsvangirai himself was repeatedly detained by police in what was seen as an attempt by ZANU-PF to restrict his ability to campaign. Furthermore, the government banned food aid. This meant that many people would have to depend on the government, and by extension ZANU-PF, for food. Many top civil society activists, election observers and members of the MDC leadership were reportedly arrested and/or assaulted. On 1 June, Arthur Mutambara, leader of the MDC-M was arrested in connection with an article he had written in 'The Standard' in April. According to the police, the article included falsehoods and was in contempt of court. On 3 June, police arrested three South Africans working for Sky News for illegal possession of broadcasting equipment. They were tried, convicted and sentenced to six months imprisonment. On 5 June, the government banned all international non-governmental organisations. On 9 June, Deputy Attorney-General Johannes Tomana announced that anyone arrested for involvement in political violence would not be granted bail. On 12 June, Tendai Biti, the MDC-T secretary general, was arrested at Harare international airport. He was charged with treason on the basis of a widely discredited MDC-T document about changing the government. The document had been confirmed as a forgery and was thought to be the work of ZANU-PF.

On 22 June, citing escalating violence, *Tsvangirai withdrew* from the run-off election. On the same day he sought refuge at the Royal Netherlands Embassy in Harare. The MDC formally submitted Tsvangirai's withdrawal to ZEC on 24 June. The government and ZEC did not recognise the withdrawal, insisting that legally he was still a candidate. The June 27 election went ahead and Mugabe won a 'resounding' victory with 85.5% of the vote against Tsvangirai's 9.3%. The MDC-T, unsurprisingly, did not recognise the election or the results. An hour after the announcement of the results, Mugabe was sworn in as president. Immediately afterwards, he called for "serious dialogue" with the opposition. On 1 July, MDC-T ruled out any possibility of a power-sharing deal with ZANU-PF.

On 5 July, *Mbeki's diplomacy* continued when he met with Mugabe together with the MDC-M leadership. MDC-T declined an invitation to attend. Following exploratory talks on 10 July, ZANU-PF and the two MDC formations, under the auspices of SADC and supported and endorsed by the AU, signed a MoU. It set out the agenda of the negotiations under four broad issues: economic, political, security and communication According to the MoU, the "dialogue [would] be completed within a period of two weeks from the date of signing of [the] MOU." The parties agreed to "refrain from negotiating through the media".

Tsvangirai, Mugabe and Mutambara met in Harare on 22 July. They expressed support for a *negotiated political settlement*. The negotiations, mediated by President Mbeki, officially began in Pretoria on 25 July. Even as the talks got under way, there was disagreement regarding their status, with the MDC-T claiming that they were no more than "talks about whether to have talks". On 25 July, it was reported that the ZANU-PF Politburo had resolved not to accept a power-sharing deal that failed to recognise Mugabe's re-election or sought to reverse the land reform programme. There was a lot of contradictory information coming from the parties during the talks. For example, on 28 July, MDC-T said that the dialogue had stalled owing to disagreement on the leadership of the government. On 29 July, Mbeki claimed the talks were going very well. On 30 July, Mugabe said that the talks were going well and that the negotiators were working towards compromise. Significantly, in a joint statement on 6 August, the parties called for an end to violence.

The SADC called for a summit in Johannesburg on 16 August. On 14 August, Tsvangirai's emergency travel documents were briefly confiscated by CIO operatives at Harare international airport. He was on his way to the *SADC summit*. The documents were quickly returned and he was able to travel. The summit ended on 17 August with no agreement. In a communiqué, the participating SADC leaders called on the parties to "conclude the negotiations as a matter of urgency to restore political stability in Zimbabwe".

On 19 August, five months after the elections, government announced that parliament would convene the following week. On 20 August, MDC-T declared that the *convening of parliament* was unacceptable, referring to it as "a clear repudiation of the Memorandum of Understanding". On 24 August, Mugabe unilaterally appointed eight resident ministers and governors as well as three non-constituency senators. The MDC-T denounced the appointments as a violation of the MoU. Members of parliament were sworn in on 25 August. In the election for the speaker of parliament, MDC-T candidate Lovemore Moyo emerged as the winner, defeating MDC-M's Paul Themba Nyathi, who was also backed by ZANU-PF. Evidence indicated that some MDC-M members voted for the MDC-T candidate. In another controversial move, on 26 November Mugabe reappointed Gideon Gono to another five-year term as governor of the Reserve Bank of Zimbabwe (RBZ). Analysts predicted that the reappointment would deepen the country's economic crisis.

On 3 September, it was reported that Mugabe had threatened to form a *cabinet* if a power-sharing deal was not signed by 4 September. On 8 September, MDC-M stated that they would not be part of a government that excluded MDC-T. Mugabe reportedly backed down from his threat. On 11 September, Tsvangirai said that a deal had been reached. Confirming this, Mbeki announced that "an agreement has been reached on all items on the agenda", pointing out that the deal would be signed in Harare on 15 September in the presence of other African leaders. On 15 September, SADC leaders witnessed the signing of the deal.

According to the *Global Political Agreement* (GPA), the Government of National Unity (GNU) would consist of a president, two vice presidents, a prime minister and two deputy prime ministers. Mugabe would be president with executive powers. He would chair cabinet and the National Security Council (NSC). Tsvangirai would be prime minister with executive powers. He would chair the council of ministers and run the day-to-day business of government. He would be a member of the NSC. Mutambara would be one of the deputy prime ministers. There would be 31 ministries: ZANU-PF 15, MDC-T 13 and MDC-M 3. The specific details on the allocation of the ministries would be worked out between the parties. Other items in the GPA included a commitment to end violence, to uphold basic freedoms, to carry out a land audit and to ensure non-partisanship in state institutions.

On 17 September, speaking to the ZANU-PF central committee, Mugabe described the agreement as a "humiliation", blaming it on the party's losses in the 29 March elections. The central committee approved the agreement. On 18 September, the three parties deliberated on the *distribution of ministries* but no agreement was reached and the case was referred to the negotiators, who met on 19 September. Again, no agreement was reached. On 4 October, the three party leaders met in Harare do discuss the issue: once more, they failed to agree. According to ZANU-PF, the disagreement centred on two ministries, home affairs and finance. Disputing this, on 5 October the MDC insisted that there were disagreement on all of the cabinet portfolios. On 9 October, Tsvangirai declared a deadlock and asked Mbeki to intervene. Mugabe, Tsvangirai and Mutambara met on 10 October and agreed to bring in Mbeki to mediate. However, on 11 October, the government mouthpiece, 'The Herald', surprisingly published an 'official' list showing the *cabinet*. The key ministries of defence, home affairs, justice, foreign affairs and local government were allotted to ZANU-PF. The MDC-T was allotted, among others, constitutional and parliamentary affairs, economic planning and investment promotion, labour and social welfare. MDC-M got education, regional integration and international cooperation, and industry and commerce. According to 'The Herald', only the finance ministry remained in dispute. The MDC-T denounced the publication of the list as "unilateral, contemptuous and outrageous". MDC-M also rejected the list dismissing it as "hallucination on the part of ZANU-PF". On 13 October, Joseph Msika and Joice Mujuru were sworn in as vice presidents, signalling that Mugabe was on the way to forming a cabinet. Protracted interparty talks between 16 and 17 October produced no agreement. The case was referred to the SADC.

On 20 October, the SADC met in Swaziland. Tsvangirai did not attend, citing the refusal of the government to issue him a proper passport. Another SADC meeting in Harare on 27 October was unsuccessful. At an *emergency SADC summit* in Johannesburg on 10 November, the leaders endorsed the immediate formation of a cabinet with shared control of the ministry of home affairs. In a significant compromise by Mugabe, the finance ministry was allocated to the MDC-T. On 12 November, the MDC-T said it would not join the government unless the outstanding issues – among them "the issue of governors, equity and allocation of key ministries" – were resolved. Interparty talks resumed in South Africa on 25 November with Mbeki as mediator. In the next few days, there were accusations and counteraccusation between Mbeki and the MDC-T with the latter calling on Mbeki to step down as mediator. On 13 December, the draft Constitutional Amendment Bill (Number 19) was published in the government gazette. In December, Tsvangirai turned down an invitation from Mugabe to be sworn in as prime minister on the basis that there were outstanding issues concerning power sharing.

As the negotiations dragged on, there was an upsurge in *state-sponsored violence*. On 13 November, the MDC-T reported that government had launched another wave of attacks on the party and human rights activists. There were increasing incidents of abductions by state security agents. The most notable case was that of Jestina Mukoko, the director of the Zimbabwe Peace Project (ZPP), which documents cases of human rights violations. A former newsreader at the Zimbabwe Broadcasting Corporation, she was abducted from her home in Norton on 3 December. For three weeks, the police claimed they did not know where she was and were treating her case as a kidnapping. One week later the high court ordered the police to look for Mukoko. Two other ZPP employees, Broderick Takawira and Pascal Gonzo, were abducted from their offices in Harare on 8 December. On 24 December, the three and other abducted activists appeared briefly in court. High court Justice Yunus Omerjee ordered the release of a number of abductees, including Pascal Gonzo. The judge also ordered Mukoko and Takawira to be released immediately to Avenues Clinic under police guard, to be given full access to their legal practitioners and relatives and to remain there until 29 December, when they were due to appear in the magistrate's court. Police disregarded the order. On 29 December, lawyers were advised that Mukoko and eight others were to be charged with allegedly recruiting or attempting to recruit individuals for training in banditry, insurgency, sabotage or terrorism. Allegedly, the abductees were severely tortured. The year ended with the individuals still incarcerated in solitary confinement at Chikurubi Maximum Security Prison.

There were many reported *abductions* in the period between October and December in various areas, particularly Mashonaland West, Manicaland, Masvingo and the Midlands provinces. In the town of Banket, on 30 October, a two year-old was abducted together with his parents and nine other MDC-T activists. At the end of the year, he remained in custody with his mother at Chikurubi Maximum Security Prison. By year's end, there were still 12 'missing' MDC officials and supporters who had reportedly been abducted.

Significantly, the year witnessed some *disturbances by soldiers.* Soldiers rioted on 28 November and 1 December allegedly in frustration over their inability to withdraw adequate amounts of their pay from the banks. On 1 December, police and rioting soldiers from the presidential guard engaged in running battles in Harare. On 16 December, the government reported that the air force chief, Air Marshal Perence Shiri, was shot on 13 December in a terrorist plot designed to destabilise the country. There was widespread speculation that the attempted assassination was a result of the feud in ZANU-PF.

There was little action on the *legislative front*. On 7 March, government gazetted the Indigenisation and Empowerment Act. It had been passed by the previous parliament and President Mugabe had assented to it. The act stipulates that black Zimbabweans must own at least 51% of the shares of every public company and all other businesses. On 28 November, the *SADC tribunal* ruled that 78 white Zimbabweans could keep their farms because Zimbabwe's land reform programme discriminated against them. However, seizures of the properties of the commercial farmers reportedly increased, as government indicated that it would disregard the ruling.

Foreign Affairs

While as a body the SADC maintained its support for Mugabe, even to the point of supporting him against Tsvangirai's demands, there was some discord in the regional body. The *Botswana* parliament unanimously adopted a motion condemning the situation in Zimbabwe. Tsvangirai, who was concerned about his security, was allowed to establish his operational base in Botswana. Reportedly, it was Ian Khama, the Botswana president, who initiated the 28 April Lusaka extraordinary SADC summit called by SADC chairman, Zambian President Levy Mwanawasa, to discuss post-election political developments in Zimbabwe. Botswana maintained its critical stance throughout the year. Significantly, Khama boycotted the 16–17 August SADC emergency summit in Johannesburg because he did not recognise Mugabe's controversial re-election. On 4 November, Zimbabwe described Botswana's calls for a fresh presidential election to solve the political crisis as "extreme" provocation. In December, Botswana's foreign minister, Phandu Skelemani, said that if neighbouring countries closed their borders with Zimbabwe, Mugabe's rule would end in a week. On 15 December, Zimbabwe's Justice Minister Patrick Chinamasa told 'The Herald' that Zimbabwe had evidence Botswana was giving military training to members of

MDC-T as part of a plot to remove Mugabe. Botswana dismissed Zimbabwe's accusation as nothing more than "distorted" and "concocted facts". On 17 December, Zimbabwe's case against Botswana was dealt a major blow when the SADC chairman, South African President Kgalema Motlanthe, disclosed that the regional bloc did not believe Zimbabwe's accusations.

Kenyan Prime Minister *Raila Odinga* was another consistent critic. Speaking at the World Economic Forum on Africa in Cape Town on 5 June, he said, "What happens in Zimbabwe is a big embarrassment for the whole continent. We cannot condone what is happening there." On 24 June, he again called the situation in Zimbabwe "a big embarrassment". On 30 June he urged the AU to "suspend [Mugabe] and send peace forces to Zimbabwe to ensure free and fair elections." In response, the Zimbabwean government said Odinga was not qualified to speak on Zimbabwe as his hands "drip of blood". On 4 December, Odinga said power-sharing in Zimbabwe was dead and it was time for African governments to oust Mugabe.

Zambian President *Levy Mwanawasa* also broke ranks with African leaders. On 22 June, he stated that the political situation in Zimbabwe was an embarrassment to the whole SADC region and Africa. He also stated that it was "scandalous for the SADC to remain silent in the light of what is happening." Other critical remarks came from Rwandan President *Paul Kagame*. On 18 June, he said that the African continent had failed the people of Zimbabwe by failing to help resolve the political crisis in that country. Referring to Zimbabwe, on 14 December Kagame said that leaders should not do wrong under the pretext of the good things they did for their countries in the past.

More critical remarks came from respected Africans. Speaking in London on 25 June, Nelson Mandela accused President Mugabe of a "tragic failure of leadership". Also on 25 June, Desmond Tutu, another consistent critic of the Zimbabwean government, labelled Mugabe a "Frankenstein" and called on other countries to intervene before the country descended into bloodshed. On 24 December,

Tutu said that the international community must use the threat of force to oust Mugabe from office. Significantly, the *SADC observer mission* concluded that the results of the run-off election "did not reflect the will of the Zimbabwean people" and judged the election as not having been carried out according to SADC standards. In July, Zimbabwe was at the top of the agenda at the *11th summit of the AU* in Egypt. The meeting, attended by Mugabe, approved a resolution calling for him to negotiate with Tsvangirai.

In December, the government allegedly barred *'The Elders'*, a group comprising former UN Secretary General Kofi Annan, former US President Jimmy Carter and women's and children's rights advocate Graça Machel, from entering Zimbabwe. The three were due to arrive on 22 November to assess the humanitarian crisis. In a statement on that date, 'The Elders' said that the government had "refused to cooperate in any way to make the visit possible". In an open letter on 13 June, 39 prominent figures in Africa, including Kofi Annan, former heads of state, and civic leaders, called for a free and fair election, stressing that this was "crucial for the interests of both Zimbabwe and Africa". On 18 June, ANC President Jacob Zuma said he was worried that Zimbabwe's presidential run-off election would not be free and fair, given the violence and and the intimidation of the opposition. Chairman of the AU Commission Jean Ping described the events as "a matter of grave concern". On 25 June, the SADC called for the election to be postponed and for "meaningful talks" to take place between ZANU-PF and the MDC, stating that "the people of Zimbabwe can solve their own problems".

Relations with the West continued to be strained. The EU, US, Australia, Canada and New Zealand maintained, renewed or strengthened targeted sanctions against Mugabe and senior ZANU-PF and government officials. The US, Britain, Australia and Sweden were among the most vocal critics of the Zimbabwean government. For its part, Zimbabwe continued to blame its problems on the West's "illegal sanctions". On April 24, Jendayi Frazer, the US assistant secretary of state for African affairs, noted that Tsvangirai had won the 29 March presidential elections and urged Mugabe to step down. On 30 June, Italy recalled its ambassador to Zimbabwe for consultations following the re-election of Mugabe. On 5 June, police and military officers detained and harassed US and British diplomats and local embassy staff who were investigating political violence in Mashonaland Central. The US described the attack as "absolutely outrageous". Britain summoned the Zimbabwean ambassador for an explanation. On 9 July, Gordon Brown described the Zimbabwean government as a "criminal cabal". He expressed doubts about the possibility of a free and fair election.

Zimbabwe continued its *'Look East' policy*. On 23 February, 'The Herald' reported that China was to lend Zimbabwe $ 42 m to buy farm equipment. The agreement was signed by Gideon Gono and the Chinese deputy commerce minister, Gao Hucheng, during a visit to Harare. Chinese firms would supply much of the equipment. Mugabe hailed China for supporting his government. On 17 April, the South African government confirmed that a *Chinese cargo ship* believed to be carrying 77 tonnes of small arms, including more than three million rounds of ammunition, AK47 assault rifles, mortars and rocket-propelled grenades, had docked in Durban. On 18 April, South Africa's high court ruled the cargo could be offloaded in Durban, but could not pass over South Africa's roads to get to Zimbabwe. Durban's dockworkers said they would not handle the cargo, fearing the arms would be used against the people. The ship then headed to the port of Luanda, Angola. It remained unclear what happened to the weapons thereafter.

On 24 June, in its first statement publicly condemning the conduct of Zimbabwe's presidential election, the *UN Security Council* unanimously blamed the Zimbabwean government for violence, intimidation and the denial of free campaigning. On 29 April, the Security Council held a session on the situation in Zimbabwe. The Zimbabwean government denounced the session as "sinister, racist and colonial", dismissing it as "a sign of desperation by the British and their MDC puppets". South Africa, which then held the Security

Council presidency, was reluctant to take up the issue of Zimbabwe. On 5 June, *UN Secretary General* Ban Ki-moon met Mugabe in Rome and announced that Mugabe had accepted a suggestion to send UN Assistant Secretary General for Political Affairs Haile Menkerios to Zimbabwe to discuss how the UN could assist in the electoral process. Ban also stressed to Mugabe "the need to stop the violence and to deploy neutral international observers". On 17 June, Menkerios met Mugabe in Harare "to discuss the technical requirements for holding the election, to see what the UN can do to help build capacity for a free and fair election." On 18 June, UN High Commissioner for Human Rights Louise Arbour announced that a member of her staff had been expelled from Zimbabwe on 17 June after spending only two days in the country. Also on that day Ban Ki-moon expressed alarm at conditions in the period leading up to the election and that, if the situation did not improve, "the legitimacy of the election outcomes would be in question". On 23 June, following Tsvangarai's withdrawal from the election, Ban Ki-moon said that the election should be postponed, pointing out that Tsvangirai's decision to withdraw was understandable given the violence against his supporters. On 12 July, Russia and China vetoed a Security Council resolution imposing *UN sanctions* on President Mugabe and his inner circle. The resolution, supported by the West, would have imposed an arms embargo on Zimbabwe and a worldwide asset freeze and travel ban on Mugabe and 13 senior government and party officials accused of orchestrating abuses in the run-off vote.

On 3 November, *Global Fund* executive director Michel Kazatchkine announced that the donor group had ordered that funds under its administration in Zimbabwe be placed under the Additional Safeguards Policy (ASP), which aims to ensure that funding is used for its intended purpose and not to benefit the government. This came after $ 6.5 m meant for the country's anti-malaria campaign mysteriously disappeared. The money was part of a $ 103 m grant from the Global Fund to Fight Aids, Tuberculosis and Malaria, $ 28.5 m of which was allocated to the health ministry for prevention and treatment of malaria. Civic groups suggested that the funds were spent by the bank to fund ZANU-PF's political activities, particularly in the run-up to the March and June elections. Zimbabwe later paid back the money.

Apart from travelling to the SADC and AU summits on Zimbabwe, Mugabe also travelled to Rome for the *UN food summit* (3 June). British and Australian ministers described his presence there as "obscene". On 19 September, with the situation still unresolved, Mugabe travelled to New York for the 63rd *UN General Assembly*, where he again blamed the West for Zimbabwe's problems.

Socioeconomic Developments

Economic indicators did not improve. According to official figures, year-on-year *inflation* surpassed 100,000% in January. By July it was 231 million per cent. Economics Intelligence Unit estimates put the GDP at $ 1.5 bn, down from $ 1.7 bn. The decline in the real GDP accelerated to –12.6%, from –5.5%. Agriculture declined by 17.5%, industry by 13% and services by 11%. The current accounts balance deteriorated from –$ 500 m to –$ 655 m, while international reserves fell from $ 120 m to $ 100 m. The total *external debt* rose from $ 4.9 bn to $ 5.3 bn. RBZ figures revealed that domestic debt was Z$ 790.6 quadrillion. On 1 August, the RBZ redenominated the currency and removed ten zeroes. The official year-end exchange rate (using the redenominated currency) was $ 1 to Z$ 200,000. In April, government devalued the Zimbabwe dollar from Z$ 250 to the US dollar to Z$ 15,000 to the US dollar. *No budget* was presented during the year. By the governor's own admission, the RBZ funded government and ZANU-PF operations by printing money.

In late November, the stock market fell sharply following *monetary policy measures* introduced by the RBZ to curb fraudulent speculative behaviour by investors who were 'buying' and 'selling' shares that were not backed by actual credit balances in their bank accounts. The government introduced a statutory requirement that from the end of November insurance firms and pension funds would have to invest between 30% and 35% of their assets in prescribed government assets. Failure to comply would result in "very serious remedial measures".

In January, government announced that it would open *'people's shops'* countrywide to provide basic commodities at affordable prices. In line with the new monetary policy, on 25 September government licensed 600 shops to sell goods in foreign currency. This was part of efforts to battle a flourishing black market trade and scarce supplies of basic commodities. This led to an increasing dollarisation of the economy, as even businesses that were not licensed began trading in foreign currency. Analysts argued this would do little to alleviate the plight of millions of Zimbabweans in the absence of radical political and economic reforms.

The *educational and health sectors* remained paralysed for most of the year due to frequent and prolonged industrial action by teachers and health personnel over salaries and working conditions. The educational and health delivery system continued to experience problems of staffing, equipment and funding. Health and educational personnel made up a substantial part of the brain drain to countries such as Australia, the UK and South Africa.

According to the Human Development Report (2007–08), Zimbabwe had an *HDI score* of 0.513 and was ranked 151st. The HIV prevalence among adults (15–49 years) was 15.6%. The proportion of people living on less than a dollar a day was 56.1%. On 19 November, the UN Consolidated Appeals Process (CAP) put out a $ 550 m consolidated appeal for Zimbabwe for 2009, citing the "the alarming degradation of Zimbabwe's economy and rise in social vulnerability [that] continued in 2008." Another failed agricultural season further increased dependence on food as well as non-food assistance and gave rise to projections that 5.1 m people would depend on *food aid* by the first quarter of 2009. The country's food needs were met through imports. Government reportedly paid Malawi $ 94 m for 400,000 tonnes of maize.

Power blackouts worsened, with some domestic and industrial areas receiving no electricity for a day or more. Zimbabwe was unable to generate all the electricity it needed and had to import power from the DR Congo, South Africa and Mozambique. The problem was compounded by the decision of Cahora Bassa (Mozambique), the main supplier, to frequently cut off supplies over unpaid debts. *Water shortages* persisted in urban areas. Power cuts and lack of foreign currency to pay for treatment chemicals were cited as the major causes. Many people, even within government and ZANU-PF circles, blamed the state-controlled Zimbabwe National Water Authority (ZINWA) for incompetence and bungling.

Migration and displacement continued, with many Zimbabweans leaving the country as political or economic refugees. According to CAP, the most evident dimension of the migration phenomenon in Zimbabwe has been the irregular migration of youths to neighbouring countries, primarily South Africa and Botswana. Because they were undocumented, the majority of Zimbabwean migrant youths were apprehended and deported back to Zimbabwe.

A *cholera outbreak* that began in Chitungwiza on 27 August spread to Harare and then to most of the country. The outbreak was blamed on the failure by ZINWA to provide uninterrupted water supplies and to collect refuse. On 30 November, government announced that cholera had killed more than 425 people and infected more than 11,000. Charging that government was trying to minimise the real death toll, the independent Zimbabwe Association of Doctors for Human Rights put the death toll at 1,000. In December, the WHO said cholera cases could balloon to 60,000 before the rainy season ended. On 8 December, the government declared the epidemic a national emergency. Government appealed for help for its hospitals, which the health minister admitted were "literally not functioning". On 11 December, Mugabe claimed that Zimbabwean doctors, with the help of "others", had "arrested" the epidemic. The statement was met with widespread ridicule and disbelief and government vigorously tried to deny that Mugabe meant that there was no more cholera in Zimbabwe. By the end of the year, the epidemic was still spreading.

Zimbabwe in 2009

The year witnessed some fundamental changes in domestic politics and the economy. The formation of the Government of National Unity (GNU) and the consequent overhaul of economic policy led to some improvements in the political and economic situation. The economy markedly improved as runaway inflation was dramatically contained. Despite persistent discord within the GNU, political violence noticeably declined after its formation. There was no major shift in foreign relations.

Domestic Politics

On 30 January, Morgan Tsvangirai, leader of the larger Movement for Democratic Change formation (MDC-T), announced that his party and the smaller MDC faction led by Arthur Mutambara (MDC-M) would enter into a *power-sharing government* with President Robert Mugabe's Zimbabwe African National Union-Patriotic Front (ZANU-PF). On 11 February, Tsvangirai was sworn in as prime minister in the GNU, along with two deputy prime ministers: Thokozani Khupe, deputy leader of the MDC-T, and Arthur Mutambara, leader of the MDC-M. In the GNU, Mugabe retained his executive position. He was chairman of the cabinet with Tsvangirai as his deputy. The *cabinet* was made up of 31 ministers, 15 from ZANU-PF and 16 from the MDC factions (13 MDC-T and 3 MDC-M). It was sworn in on 13 February. Mugabe also chaired the National Security Council, a body comprising security services chiefs and Tsvangirai. Tsvangirai chaired the council of ministers, which would oversee the work of cabinet. Its members included all cabinet ministers. Contention regarding the ministry of home affairs, under which the police falls, was resolved by having two 'co-ministers', Kembo Mohadi from ZANU-PF, who was also the sitting

 | DOI:10.1163/9789004404335_003

minister, and Giles Mutsekwa from the MDC-T. The ministry of finance, another contentious issue, was given to MDC-T secretary-general Tendai Biti. The GNU established the Joint Monitoring and Implementation Committee to monitor the implementation of the power-sharing agreement. The 12-member committee (with four members from each of the three parties to the agreement) would have three chairpersons, one from each of the parties.

There were persistent doubts as to whether the GNU would work. Critics considered the MDC to be a junior partner. Mugabe retained control of the judiciary as well as the military and security apparatus, with the MDC-T having charge mainly of the development and service ministries. The GNU was seen as no more than a transitional arrangement leading to a new constitution and new election at some point in the future. It was characterised by *disputes*. On 25 February, Tsvangirai 'cancelled' the previous day's unilateral appointment of permanent secretaries by Mugabe. On 10 April, Mugabe, again unilaterally, moved the communication portfolio from the MDC-T – controlled ministry of information communication technology to the ZANU-PF – controlled ministry of transport, which would become the ministry of transport and communication. Tsvangirai swiftly declared the unilateral move "null and void". Mugabe uncharacteristically backed down. By the end of the year, there were still some *unresolved issues*, including the appointment of provincial governors, the swearing in of Roy Bennett as deputy agriculture minister, and contention over the attorney general and governor of the Reserve Bank of Zimbabwe (RBZ), whom the MDC-T wanted dismissed. On its part, ZANU-PF insisted that no concessions would be made unless the MDC-T successfully called for the lifting of the 'illegal' sanctions imposed by its Western partners. In addition, ZANU-PF supporters continued *farm invasions*. By the end of the year, mounting violence was reported against the remaining 400 white-owned commercial farms. It came as no surprise when Tsvangirai admitted on 30 May that the GNU had made little progress.

On 16 October, Tsvangirai announced that the MDC-T had disengaged from the GNU over the treatment of *Roy Bennett*. The MDC-T treasurer had been appointed to the position of deputy minister of agriculture, but was arrested on 13 February hours before the ministers in the unity government were to be sworn in. He was initially charged with treason; the charges were later changed to attempting to commit terrorism, banditry and sabotage. While the police insisted the arrest was not politically motivated, the charges were widely interpreted as political persecution and an expression of Mugabe's contempt for the GNU. Tsvangirai said all the issues outstanding with regard to the power-sharing agreement had to be dealt with before the MDC would work with ZANU-PF. He described ZANU-PF as "an unreliable and unrepentant partner in the transitional government". The party embarked on a nationwide *consultation process* on the future of the GNU, which amounted to a veritable referendum on the GNU. On 5 November, Tsvangirai announced that he had suspended the disengagement from the GNU, adding that ZANU-PF had 30 days to meet the issues still outstanding from the 2008 Global Political Agreement (GPA). This did not happen. On 23 December, Mugabe, Mutambara and Tsvangirai held a joint press conference. They admitted that they still had minor differences, but insisted that the GNU was not going to collapse.

Controversies about *politically motivated violence* dogged the GNU. On 24 February, the MDC released a statement criticising the arrest and detention of its members and civil society activists. On 2 March, Jestina Mukoko, the director of the Zimbabwe Peace Project, and several other MDC-T supporters were granted bail after spending three months in detention; they still faced treason charges. On 28 September, the Supreme Court ruled in their favour, quashing all charges against them because they had been tortured by state security agents. After his inauguration, Tsvangirai had called for an end to human rights abuses and political violence. Levels of violence dropped, though violence reportedly increased in rural areas in the second half of the year. It was speculated that ZANU-PF tried to whittle down the MDC's parliamentary majority by causing the arrest of seven MDC-T MPs to enforce by-elections in rural constituencies with the aim of regaining a parliamentary majority by having its own candidates elected. This strategy might not have been successful, as an *opinion poll* taken in May by the Zimbabwe Mass Public Opinion Institute, showed support for ZANU-PF among voters was less than 10%, while the MDC-T commanded 57%.

On 12 April, in line with the GPA, the GNU set up a 25-member parliamentary select committee to spearhead the drafting of a new *constitution* within 18 months. The constitution was to be completed by February 2010 and followed by a national referendum five months later. The process ran into problems as sections of civil society, led by the National Constitutional Assembly, denounced the move and called for a people-driven constitution-making process. Even the pro-MDC-T Zimbabwe Congress of Trade Unions (CTU) warned against restricting the process to politicians. On 22 April, two legislators, one from ZANU-PF (Paul Mangwana) and the other from the MDC-T (Douglas Mwonzora), were appointed to co-chair the select committee. There was some uncertainty about the positions of the 'Kariba Draft', secretly negotiated between the MDC formations and ZANU-PF in September 2007, with ZANU-PF insisting it was to be the basis of the new constitution, a position rejected by the MDC-T national executive on 23 June. On 13 July, a conference to draw up the new constitution descended into chaos as riot police broke up clashes between rival delegates. ZANU-PF supporters were blamed for violently disrupting the meeting. This underscored the tensions within the GNU. Interviews for *constitutional commissions* were conducted by the parliament's Committee on Standing Rules and Orders (CSRO). Interviews for the Zimbabwe Media Commission (ZMC) were held on 12 August; for the new Independent Zimbabwe Electoral Commission on 28 September; and for the Human Rights Commission on 12 October. Controversy was not lacking concerning the interview procedure and the final shortlists submitted to

Mugabe. On 22 September, the CSRO announced they had been advised of a constitutional clause indicating that members of the Anti-Corruption Commission would be appointed by the president "in consultation with" the CSRO.

On 1 October, the state daily reported that George Charamba, secretary for Media, Information and Publicity (MIP), had announced a list of board members for six *media institutions* that fell under the ministry. The boards concerned were the Broadcasting Authority of Zimbabwe, Zimpapers, Zimbabwe Broadcasting Holdings, Transmedia, Kingstons and New Ziana. The appointments were made "unilaterally" by MIP minister Webster Shamu. On the boards were Charles Utete, former secretary to the cabinet, and Tafataona Mahoso, notoriously known as the media hangman, who had muzzled the media during his tenure as the Media and Information Commission (MIC) chairman. Tsvangirai and Mutambara, as well as deputy MIP minister Jameson Timba, dismissed the appointments as illegal, unprocedural and invalid.

There was some relaxation of *media restrictions*. On 29 July, Shamu announced that CNN and the BBC were permitted to return to live broadcasting from Zimbabwe after an eight-year ban. There were calls on the government to lift the ban on newspapers such as the 'Daily News', 'Daily News on Sunday', the 'Tribune' and 'Weekly Times' by speedily processing their licenses as agreed under the GPA. There were also calls to repeal repressive legislation such as the Access to Information and Protection of Privacy Act and Broadcasting Services Act to allow the entry of new players in both the print and broadcasting sector. In July, a special committee, set up in September 2008 to review the MIC's refusal to grant a licence to the banned 'Daily News' and 'Daily News on Sunday' newspapers, said it was satisfied that Associated Newspapers of Zimbabwe (ANZ) had complied with the provisions of the Access to Information and Protection of Privacy Act. The chairman of the committee wrote to ANZ's lawyers on 30 July advising them "to contact the relevant authority for their licence". However, ANZ would have to wait for an unknown period for its licence as the successor body to the MIC, the ZMC, was still to be constituted.

On 12 December, Mugabe was re-elected as leader at a depleted *ZANU-PF party congress* in Harare. He had already been endorsed as the ZANU-PF candidate for the 2013 presidential elections. The congress almost failed to take place as the party struggled to raise funds for the event. The Mujuru faction outflanked the rival Mnangagwa faction, which had been widely expected to eclipse its rival, by securing most of the influential positions. Jonathan Moyo, the former information and publicity minister who had been re-admitted into ZANU-PF, was elected to the central committee. On 30 June, former finance minister and presidential candidate Simba Makoni launched a *new political party*, Mavambo.Kusile.Dawn, insisting it was an alternative to the GNU. It was believed he would draw moderates from ZANU-PF, but this did not materialise.

All three parties in the GNU had their own *internal problems*. ZANU-PF was still riven by splits between the factions rallying behind Mujuru, Mnangagwa and Mugabe. The power struggles apparently intensified following the death of Vice President Joseph Msika on 4 August. The MDC formations had their fair share of problems: the MDC-T was not united on how to deal with their frustrations with the GNU and the MDC-M had no less than three factions claiming leadership of the party.

On 2 October, the Swiss multinational *Nestlé* announced it would stop buying milk from a farm owned by the president's wife, Grace Mugabe. Nestlé apparently made the decision because of negative attention and boycott threats. The decision prompted a backlash from ZANU-PF loyalists, including senior party and government officials, among them Minister of Youth Development, Indigenisation and Empowerment Savior Kasukuwere. On 23 December, Nestlé suspended operations, citing harassment and the security of its employees.

Foreign Affairs

Relations with most African countries and organisations remained largely friendly, with the majority of leaders supporting the GNU. This is not surprising as SADC and the AU are the original guarantors of the GPA. Throughout the year, the MDC-T continued to refer unresolved matters about the GNU and GPA to SADC and the AU, with little success.

SADC continued its efforts to make the GNU work. On 24 March, it was announced that the venue for a SADC extraordinary summit of heads of state, which was set to discuss possible financial aid to help steer Zimbabwe's economic recovery, had been changed to Mbabane, Swaziland and would take place on 30 March. The meeting had originally been scheduled for Cape Town. When it finally took place, the summit, which Mugabe attended, noted the GNU's Short-Term Emergency Recovery Programme (STERP) to guide efforts towards economic and social recovery. Among the resolutions, the summit urged member states "to support Zimbabwe to implement STERP, in the form of budget support, lines of credit, joint ventures and toll manufacturing"; developed countries "to lift all forms of sanctions against Zimbabwe"; donors, international financial institutions and the international community in general "to support Zimbabwe and provide it with the necessary financial support for its timely economic recovery"; and "established a Committee comprising the SADC Troika of Ministers of Finance to coordinate SADC support to Zimbabwe['s] recovery process". In response to Zimbabwe's request for an $ 8.5 bn economic recovery package, SADC agreed to support Zimbabwe, but without any firm pledges except from South Africa. On 30 October, following a SADC foreign ministers' *review of the GPA*, Mugabe was forced to accept the January SADC summit communiqué, which had eventually led to the formation of the GNU, as a binding document. The communiqué, which he had originally refused to recognise as part of the GPA, stipulated among other things that the appointments of the RBZ governor and the attorney general would be dealt with by the inclusive government after its inauguration. On 5 November, Mugabe, Tsvangirai and Mutambara attended a *SADC summit* in Maputo, which sought to prevent the collapse of the GNU. It was organised by SADC's Politics, Defence and Security Troika (Mozambique, Swaziland and Zambia) and was chaired by Mozambican President Armando Guebuza.

In a judgement made available on 3 March, high court judge Justice Anne-Mary Gowora ruled that the 2008 judgment of the *SADC Tribunal*, declaring the land invasions illegal did not apply and could not be enforced in Zimbabwe unless parliament ratified the protocol that set up the tribunal. On 2 November, the official 'Herald' newspaper announced that Zimbabwe had formally withdrawn its membership of the tribunal, throwing into disarray pending cases in which white farmers challenged the legality of the country's land reform programme. Zimbabwe announced it had withdrawn from any legal proceedings by the tribunal until the establishment of the court was ratified by at least two-thirds of the bloc's membership, as required under SADC rules and procedures. Reacting to the move, SADC Executive Secretary Tomaz Salamao said the repudiation had been referred to the ministers of justice of the regional bloc's member nations, who had been asked to provide legal guidance to SADC heads of state.

It was widely anticipated that the appointment of Jacob Zuma as president of *South Africa* would change former president Thabo Mbeki's controversial 'quiet diplomacy'. Although Zuma actively sought to resolve the problems in the GNU, he was later criticised for being pro-ZANU-PF. On 27 August, Zuma made his first official visit to Zimbabwe, where he officially opened the 99th Harare Agricultural Show. He urged the GNU partners to get along with each other, but the visit appeared to have little impact. At the summit in Maputo on 5 November, SADC leaders gave the GNU coalition partners 15 to 30 days to sort out their differences, but the deadline passed without any meeting between the negotiators. On 23 November, it was announced that Zuma had postponed his visit to assess Zimbabwe's troubled power-sharing agreement, as his advisors had expressed impatience over delays in concluding the talks. The South African government stated that it now expected the issues to be dealt with by 5 December, but that 'deadline' also passed. Apparently in an effort to reduce waves of Zimbabwean asylum seekers, South Africa announced on 4 May that Zimbabwean citizens could travel there on free 90-day visitor's permits and apply to do casual work during their stay.

In what was interpreted as an attempt to win over SADC leaders, *Tsvangirai* visited the DRC, South Africa and Angola in October. On 23 October, he announced that DRC President and SADC Chairman Jospeh Kabila would visit Harare to mediate the crisis bedevilling the GNU. Kabila, seen as a Mugabe ally, visited on 1 November without significant results. On 19 November, Tsvangirai left for Morocco and Libya. He briefed the Libyan leader, then chairman of the AU, who had invited him.

Relations with *Botswana* remained tense. While the MDC-T had good relations with the country, ZANU-PF remained hostile as Botswana remained critical of the Mugabe administration. On 15 March, Botswana's foreign affairs minister said no evidence of terrorist training camps had been presented to Gaborone to support the allegations made by Mugabe's government in September 2008. Botswana rejected "the unsubstantiated allegations which were made and are clearly nothing more than an exercise to engage in acts of intimidation and harassment of the innocent people of Zimbabwe".

Other international visits included a state visit by President Rupiah Banda of *Zambia*, who was invited to open the Zimbabwe International Trade fair in Bulawayo on 2 May. He donated 9,000 tonnes of maize. In July, Mugabe visited Zambia. He was guest of honour at a ceremony to commemorate the establishment of the Mukuni Ng'ombe dynasty. In mid-November, a delegation from

Brazil visited and met Vice President Joice Mujuru on 17 November. Led by Brazil's under secretary for Africa and Asia in the ministry of external affairs, the delegation stated that Brazil wanted to strengthen economic ties with Zimbabwe and to partner the country in development projects. On 13 August, the deputy minister of foreign affairs of *Iran* began a five-day official visit as part of the two countries' move to implement agreements signed during Mugabe's visit to Iran in 2006.

Relations with the West hardly improved. Mugabe and ZANU-PF officials continued to blame Zimbabwe's woes on 'illegal' western sanctions and the MDC-M seemed to agree with this position. Tsvangirai and his MDC-T labelled the sanctions "restrictive measures", which did not go down well with ZANU-PF. Significantly, on 5 March, Tsvangirai called for the "restrictive measures" to be lifted.

Zimbabwe actively sought *international aid* to revive the ailing economy. On 11 January, Mugabe dispatched Foreign Minister Simbarashe Mbengegwi to Tripoli to deliver a letter to the Libyan leader. This was seen as part of a begging campaign to help Zimbabwe out of its economic meltdown. Paul Mangwana, the acting information minister, confirmed that Harare was seeking an economic package from "friends in Southern Africa and other parts of the world who are sympathetic". The 'friends' included Russia, Iran and China. On 5 June, Tsvangirai started a three-week tour of Europe and the United States, ostensibly to drum up financial aid for his unity government. The visit took him to the Netherlands, France, Sweden, Britain, Belgium, Germany, Denmark and the US, where he met President Obama. The visit did not bring significant financial aid from the largely sceptical Western governments. Tsvangirai raised $ 150 m in fresh aid pledges to be disbursed through NGOs. The 'Herald' newspaper ridiculed and condemned the visit. A rival ZANU-PF mission, let by Defence Minister Emmerson Mnangagwa visited Asia and Russia. At the end of June, Tsvangirai announced that *China* had extended credit lines amounting to $ 950 m.

On 30 January, the new *United States* administration voiced scepticism over the power-sharing agreement, stating that US aid would be given only when a representative government was in place. In contrast to the Bush administration, however, State Department spokesman Robert Wood did not call for Mugabe's removal. Throughout the year, the US government focused on humanitarian aid rather than development aid and lifting sanctions. On 5 March, Obama announced that US 'targeted' sanctions aimed at Mugabe and members of his government would continue for another year.

On 26 January, EU *sanctions* on Zimbabwe's leadership were tightened. The EU condemned Mugabe's government for its "ongoing failure to address the most basic economic and social needs of its people". The EU's General Affairs Council extended the restrictions for another year. Added to the list were more than 60 other "persons and entities that are actively associated with the violence or human rights infringements of the regime". According to a letter made public on 28 May, the EU was not yet ready to establish normal ties with Zimbabwe or resume aid, despite a "positive evolution" in politics. The letter was addressed to John Kaputin, secretary general of the ACP. Sanctions were also renewed by Australia, New Zealand and Switzerland. On 15 September, Australia announced it was considering easing a ban on high-level contacts with Zimbabwe, but Foreign Minister Stephen Smith added that it was too soon to end the targeted sanctions. Australia would, however, contribute an extra A$ 8 m in aid to Zimbabwe to fund emergency food supplies, agriculture projects and education.

Zimbabwe's relationships with regional and multilateral *financial institutions* did not change significantly. As of April 2009, Zimbabwe owed an estimated $ 1.24 bn in debt arrears to the World Bank, the AfDB, and the IMF. On 9 March, in response to a request from Zimbabwe, the IMF sent its first delegation to Zimbabwe in two years. The two-week mission was meant to assess the situation and to meet senior officials of the GNU, including Finance Minister Tendai Biti. Zimbabwe's IMF arrears were estimated at $ 130 m, making the prospect of anything coming out of the Article IV consultation slim. The AfDB was owed some $ 460 m and had stopped lending to Zimbabwe until the debt was repaid. On 22 May, the World Bank announced that the right conditions had not yet been created for the institution to re-engage on a fully-fledged economic development programme with Zimbabwe. By then Zimbabwe owed $ 673 m to the World Bank in debt arrears. Humanitarian assistance provided to help the poor was being channelled through NGOs and aid agencies.

Mugabe attended the 13th Ordinary Session of the *AU*, which took place in Sirte, Libya, from 24 June to 3 July. This was interpreted as a clear indication that it was still he who held the power in the GNU. Mugabe also attended the 64th Ordinary Session of the *UN*. In his address on 26 September, he underlined the need for the UN to truly serve the interest of all states and predictably condemned sanctions on Zimbabwe and the embargo on Cuba.

Socioeconomic Developments

There were some dramatic improvements in *key economic indicators*. Consumer price inflation closed the year at about 92.3%. Economist Intelligence Unit estimates put the nominal GDP at $ 1.63 bn, down from $ 1.5 bn in 2008. The official 2010 budget estimated the GDP as at October at $ 5.179 bn. GDP grew by 4.7%. The current accounts balance marginally deteriorated from –$ 584 m to –$ 590 m, while international reserves declined from $ 96 m in 2008 to $ 91 m. As at 31 December, the grand total of all external debt stock, including $ 4.244 bn of arrears, was $ 5.670 bn. Domestic borrowings for the year amounted to a cumulative total of $ 53.9 m.

On 19 March, the GNU launched an interim economic blue print to resuscitate the battered economy. At the launch of the plan, dubbed *STERP*, Finance Minister Biti stated that Zimbabwe's economic recovery was predicated on increasing production capacity.

The general idea behind the programme was to boost capacity in agriculture and other key sectors such as mining, tourism, construction and public works. Biti said the biggest hurdle to implementing the recovery programme was that it required outside financial assistance, which unfortunately had not yet started coming. Over $ 5 bn were required. The emergency short-term stabilisation programme would run from February to December.

Two budgets were produced for the year. One, the Z$ 66.5 quintillion ($ 1.7 bn) 'ZANU-PF budget', was presented by the then acting finance minister, Patrick Chinamasa, on 29 January. The second, which became the official GNU budget, was presented on 18 March by Biti, the new finance minister. Slashing the 'ZANU-PF budget', Biti revised spending and revenue estimates to $ 1 bn. The currency had been redenominated in January. Hyperinflation at well over 1 bn% made the local currency worthless. In the new budget, the Zimbabwe dollar ('Zimdollar') was dumped as the trading currency and replaced by a *multiple currency regime.* The country started trading mainly in the US dollar, the South African rand and the Botswana pula. The move appeared to cause some discord in the GNU. On several occasions Mugabe hinted that the Zimdollar would be reintroduced. In November, he said, "The use of multiple currencies is not helping our people much as the money is difficult to secure. We will be re-introducing our own currency by end of the year." The RBZ governor at times favoured the return of the local currency. Biti, the MDC-T finance minister, said he would resign if the Zimdollar returned.

The dumping of the Zimdollar has been largely credited with bringing sanity to the economy. Goods that had vanished from stores became available. The improvement in the general *macroeconomic environment* and the consequent increase in capacity utilisation contributed to price stability, which characterised the economy for the rest of the year. Inflation was dramatically reduced. According to RBZ figures, by November monthly price increases (annualised) had dropped to –1.19%.

On 2 December, Biti presented the *2010 budget* to parliament, proposing expenditure of $ 2.25 bn against revenues of $ 44 bn for an $ 810 m deficit, which would have to be filled by drawing down IMF credits or through loans or grants. Biti projected a 2010 economic expansion of 7%, with inflation for 2010 projected at 5.1%. He also proposed a budget deficit equal to 14.6% of GDP. Total funding requested from ministries and government departments totalled some $ 12 bn, against the projected revenue of $ 1.44 bn, indicating the scale of need.

Despite some decline in the downward slide, the *education and heath* delivery systems continued to experience problems of staffing, equipment and funding. As in recent years, health and educational personnel made up a substantial part of the brain drain to countries such as Australia, the United Kingdom and South Africa. Industrial action and threats of industrial action arising out of salary disputes, particularly by doctors, nurses and teachers, were a constant feature throughout the year, further compromising these sectors. In March, the Zimbabwe CTU demanded a national minimum wage of $ 454 a month from June. At the same time, teachers demanded a monthly wage of $ 2,300. The government's wage package for civil servants was $ 100.

Zimbabwe continued to lose skilled manpower through *migration*, mainly to Commonwealth countries. In its 2009 Migration Initiatives Appeal, the International Organization for Migration claimed that Zimbabwe was "a source, transit and destination country for trafficking in persons for the purposes of forced labour, sexual exploitation and domestic servitude". The country was home to "mobile and vulnerable" populations. The relaxation of visa requirements for Zimbabwean citizens travelling to South Africa was expected to have significant effects. This would hardly reduce the number of Zimbabwean migrants, but the anticipated dramatic increase in the flow of Zimbabweans crossing into South Africa did not materialise.

The *cholera epidemic* continued to spread at the beginning of the year. WHO figures released on 2 February showed that more than 62,000 people had been infected in the outbreak, which led to more than 3,200 deaths. Throughout the year, *electricity and water shortages* became widespread in urban areas. Power cuts were attributed to Zimbabwe being cut off by South African and Mozambican suppliers for failing to settle outstanding debts. Water shortages, a contributory factor to the cholera epidemic, were attributed to shortages of power and purifying chemicals, and ageing plant and equipment, all of which were explained as being the result of a lack of foreign currency and sub-economic tariffs.

In September, new estimates released by the ministry of health and child welfare showed that Zimbabwe's adult *HIV* prevalence rate was continuing its downward trend with a fall from 14.1% in 2008 to 13.7%. Earlier, in August, Zimbabwe had received $ 37.9 m from the Global Fund, which decided to bypass Zimbabwe's National AIDS Council as the principal recipient of existing and future grants after the RBZ had admitted in 2008 to diverting over $ 7 m from the Global Fund's Round 5 grant earmarked for scaling up the national antiretroviral programme.

According to the treasury, after the introduction of stable multiple currencies and supportive measures such as cash budgeting, prices of goods and the services – and with them the *cost of living* – stabilised considerably during the year. From January to October, month-on-month inflation had been oscillating between −3.1% and 1%.

There were marginal improvements in *food security*. However, the WFP reported that recent hyperinflation, an acute shortage of basic supplies and a series of very poor harvests had led to serious food shortages and acute food insecurity. Increasing levels of vulnerability were compounded by the collapsing economy, very high unemployment (estimated at over 80%), and a high HIV/AIDS prevalence rate. This situation necessitated large-scale humanitarian food assistance operations. The maize harvest amounted to 1.14 m tonnes, more than 1.3 times the 2008 level. But Zimbabwe still faced a cereal shortfall of around 677,000 tonnes. A FAO/WFP assessment estimated that around 2.8 m people, mostly in rural areas, might need humanitarian assistance before the 2010 harvest.

Zimbabwe's *diamond industry* faced problems. In June, HRW published a report detailing military activity in the diamond fields. In July, a sensitive report by the Kimberly Process (Diamond) Certification System (KPCS) gave details of atrocities committed by the army that by then had left about 200 dead in the contentious Chiadzwa diamond field in the Marange district of Manicaland Province. The report noted "unacceptable and horrific violence against civilians by authorities in and around Chiadzwa" and recommended a six-month suspension of the import and export of rough diamonds. The government ignored the recommendations and did not release the report. In September, Zimbabwe Lawyers for Human Rights demanded the official release of the report, which was already freely available on the internet, and the government's compliance with its recommendations. On 26 November, the Rapaport Diamond Trading Network (RapNet), the global network of companies that supports the development of free, fair and competitive global diamond markets, announced it had banned trading in diamonds from the Marange fields because of reported human rights violations.

In a move that spread anxiety among investors, the government seized assets of the stock exchange-listed *Meikles group* under a controversial anti-corruption law. An Extraordinary Government Gazette published on 11 September, announced that the government had frozen the assets of four companies linked to the Meikles family – Kingdom Meikles, Tanganda Tea Company (Private) Limited, Thomas Meikles Centre (Private) Limited and Murlis Investments (Private) Limited – and commenced investigations into allegations of externalising huge sums of foreign currency levelled against these entities.

Zimbabwe in 2010

The year was dominated by developments in the Government of National Unity (GNU) characterised by contradictory statements on the state of the coalition and a love-hate relationship between the three principals to the Global Political Agreement (GPA). The economy continued its tenuous improvement. Some political tensions persisted and incidents of political violence were reported, with the two major parties predictably claiming to be victims and habitually blaming each other. With no let-up in Western criticism of the government, while Zimbabwe's friends maintained their support, the foreign affairs scene remained largely unchanged.

Domestic Politics

The GNU appeared to be riddled with persistent tensions, obvious animosity and endless disagreements. On 29 January, the larger Tsvangirai-led Movement for Democratic Change formation (MDC-T) asserted that internal negotiations with ZANU-PF on the *Global Political Agreement* (GPA) "were as good as dead". It claimed that, "the inclusive government is now in grave danger of collapse". According to the MDC, only the intervention of South Africa's President Jacob Zuma and SADC could save the shaky coalition. This came in the wake of an unsurprising ZANU-PF politburo decision that there would be no further concessions on the GPA before the lifting of Western sanctions. In response to this, Prime Minister and leader of the MDC-T Morgan Tsvangirai called in February for fresh elections, a suggestion rejected by both ZANU-PF and MDC-M, the smaller MDC faction, then led by Arthur Mutambara. For the rest of the year, the parties were still deadlocked on some key points: President Robert Mugabe's refusal to reverse his unilateral appointment of Johannes Tomana as attorney general, and Gideon Gono as

 | DOI:10.1163/9789004404335_004

the Reserve Bank of Zimbabwe (RBZ) governor; his refusal to swear in MDC-T treasurer-general Roy Bennett as deputy minister of agriculture; and his refusal to reform the security sector, perceived as an extension of ZANU-PF that was used to continue acts of repression to ostensibly tip the balance against the other two parties.

Tensions in the GNU escalated when, on 20 May, Mugabe unilaterally appointed a new Supreme Court judge and four High Court judges, without the knowledge of the other two principals. Retired Brigadier-General George Chiweshe, the former chairperson of the Zimbabwe Electoral Commission (ZEC), which ran the contentious 2008 elections and was seen to have kept Mugabe in power by withholding election results, was appointed as the new judge president of the High Court, following the elevation of Rita Makarau to the Supreme Court. Reacting to the unilateral appointments, the MDC-T announced that they were "gob smacked" pointing out that this was "another act in addition to the catalogue of GPA violations and ... Mugabe's unilateralism". Not surprisingly, domestic criticism of the GNU did not diminish throughout the year. However, in an unexpected turn of events, Prime Minister Morgan Tsvangirai claimed, on 11 September, that he and Mugabe had agreed to hold *elections in 2011* and that whoever lost should not challenge the outcome of the polls. This was not a popular strategy within the MDC-T.

On 7 October, Tsvangirai publicly rejected Mugabe's *unilateral (re)appointment* of provincial governors, judges, ambassadors and other public office-holders as unconstitutional and illegal, claiming that Mugabe had acted in breach of the GPA. On 25 November, Tsvangirai filed a lawsuit against Mugabe, alleging that he had violated the constitution and the power-sharing agreement. Tsvangirai sought the annulment of Mugabe's unilateral appointment of ten provincial governors, which, he maintained, had intentionally violated the constitution. He pointed out that the power-sharing agreement required the president to consult with the prime minister before making key appointments, and that Mugabe had not abided by this provision in this latest catalogue of alleged GPA violations.

In December, documents published by the whistleblower website, *Wikileaks*, were latched onto by Mugabe's supporters to 'prove' that Tsvangirai was a puppet of the West and to cast doubts on his performance, personality and competence. The documents supposedly exposed the MDC-T's complicity in calling for sanctions on Zimbabwe and diplomats' somewhat unflattering assessment of Tsvangirai's qualities as a leader. In contrast, negative reports on ZANU-PF and Mugabe were not picked up by the state-controlled press, although they were extensively used by critics of Mugabe to denigrate him.

Another sign of discord within the GNU were the delays and disagreements that characterised the formulation of the *new constitution*, which, by the beginning of the year, was already five months behind schedule. On 21 May, it was announced that the outreach programme to gather the public's views on Zimbabwe's proposed new constitution would begin on 15 June and end on 15 September. ZANU-PF's Paul Mangwana, one of the three chairpersons of the Constitutional Parliamentary Committee (COPAC), announced that UNDP had released $ 7.1 m of the $ 8.2 m needed for the exercise. The programme was finally launched on 16 June. From the outset, the campaign was plagued with problems, including persistent interparty squabbles, violence (blamed on ZANU-PF), logistics and finance. NGOs monitoring the process claimed that intimidation and violence were discouraging participation, especially in rural areas where ZANU-PF was accused of coaching people on what to say and threatening those who spoke without the party's authorisation and/or against the party's position. Confirming *deep divisions* in the formulation of the new constitution, on 5 October, Tsvangirai described the process as a "circus", accusing the military of intimidation during outreach meetings. The MDC-T demanded that at least 1,100 outreach debates should be held again. There were, however, reports that in some areas the outreach programme was reaching and gathering views from marginalised groups including youth and women. Significantly, on 1 October, COPAC began consulting the Zimbabwean diaspora in South Africa. Following the finalisation of the outreach meetings in October, COPAC began compiling data ahead of thematic committee discussions and announced, on 12 October, that the drafting of the proposed constitution would be done in January 2011, with a second all-stakeholders conference scheduled for 31 March 2011. On the same day, it was announced that parliament had set 30 June 2011 as the date for the referendum.

Despite the problems within the GNU, there was progress on some issues agreed on in the GPA. On 1 April, Mugabe swore in the ZEC and the Zimbabwe Human Rights Commission (ZHRC). This was widely seen as a step towards *implementing the GPA*. The first chairperson of the ZHRC was Reginald Austin, a law professor and former head of the legal affairs division of the Commonwealth. Simpson Mutambanengwe, a former Supreme Court judge, then serving as acting chief justice in the Namibian Supreme Court, was sworn in as the head of the ZEC.

Political violence and other *human rights violations* reportedly declined but did not disappear altogether. On 19 May, the MDC-T accused members of the Zimbabwe National Army of leading a campaign of violence and intimidation in Manicaland province. According to the party, soldiers, with the help of war veterans and ZANU-PF supporters, were using threats and physical violence ahead of the delayed constitutional outreach exercise. Alleged disappearances, illegal arrests and physical violence were reported, especially in rural areas.

There were significant developments in *media freedom*. On 26 May, the Zimbabwe Media Commission issued licences to four daily newspapers, including 'The Daily News', which had been banned by the then Media and Information Commission in 2003. Other dailies registered were Alpha Media's 'Newsday', Modus Publications' 'Daily Gazette' and 'The Mail', owned by an unknown company called Fruitlink. Many read this development as promising to change the media landscape, which had seen partisan state-controlled papers monopolising the dailies sector. Other commentators were either guarded or sceptical and wondered whether the country could sustain so many daily newspapers.

The *rule of law* was as usual a contentious issue. On 25 March, the Zimbabwe Human Rights Organisation (ZimRights) was forced to abandon a photo exhibition in Harare highlighting human rights violations during the violent June 2008 presidential run-off elections. This came after police had attempted to re-seize photographs they had earlier returned following a High Court ruling declaring the seizure illegal and ordering the police to return the material. The High Court had ruled that there was no basis in law for the police to shut down the exhibition. On 29 March, an attorney announced that police in Bulawayo had shut down an art exhibit exploring violence blamed on the government. The artist, Owen Maseko, was arrested for incitement.

On 10 March, *Roy Bennett*, the MDC-T appointed deputy minister of agriculture whom Mugabe had adamantly refused to swear in citing the criminal case outstanding against him, was unexpectedly acquitted on charges of possessing arms for purposes of terrorism, banditry and sabotage. He had been arrested in February 2009, when the GNU was being sworn in. Justice Chinembiri Bhunu ruled that the state had failed to prove there were reasonable grounds for a prosecution. Johannes Tomana, the controversial attorney general seen by many as a ZANU-PF functionary, told journalists after the ruling that he was satisfied by the judgment, appearing to suggest he would not appeal against the acquittal. However, on 12 May, he filed a Chamber Application in the Supreme Court seeking leave to appeal against the ruling. By the end of the year, the case was yet to be heard.

Some disenchantment with the GNU's performance was evident in February, when civil servants, spearheaded by teachers, embarked on a series of *industrial actions* that were to recur sporadically throughout the year. They were demanding a 400% pay rise. The former trade union leader Tsvangirai was not of particular help when he remarked that civil servants should not complain about the salaries they were receiving. On 14 February, the Public Service Commission declared the strike illegal. Throughout the year, threats of more labour unrest either loomed or materialised.

There was a lot of activity on intra-party politics. Amid reports of *power struggles in the MDC-T*, on 22 June, Tsvangirai dropped four MDC-T ministers from the cabinet in a reshuffle he described as strengthening the performance of his party in the inclusive government. Giles Mutsekwa was replaced as home affairs co-minister by Theresa Makone; he was moved to housing and social amenities. Elias Mudzuri, a senior party member, was dropped from the ministry of energy and power development (MEPD). Also dropped was Fidelis Mhashu, who was minister of national housing and social amenities. Both Mudzuri and Mhashu were deployed to party duties. Evelyn Masaiti, formerly deputy minister of women's affairs, gender and community development, and Thamasanqa Mahlangu, formerly deputy minister of youth, indigenisation and empowerment (YIE), were also dropped. Tapiwa Mashakada took over the economic planning and investment promotion ministry from Elton Mangoma, who was redeployed to the MEPD. Gift Chimanikire, who had rejoined the larger MDC formation from the smaller faction, was promoted to deputy minister for mines and mining development. Other new deputy ministers were Obert Gutu (justice and legal affairs) and Tongai Matutu (YIE). Throughout the year, there were reports of disgruntlement within the MDC-T, with Tsvangirai's so-called 'kitchen cabinet' of advisers getting most of the criticism for misleading him and blocking access to him. In what was interpreted as an indication of dissatisfaction over Tsvangirai's leadership style, the MDC-T resolved in August that he would no longer make senior appointments without first having consulted the party's National Standing Committee.

The inter-faction power struggles within ZANU-PF reportedly continued. On 11 November, the 'Zimbabwe Independent' reported that Mugabe had crushed *dissent in ZANU-PF*. This came amid speculative reports that Mugabe's leadership of ZANU-PF and the country had been coming under serious challenge, particularly from within the politburo. The paper quoted ZANU-PF insiders as saying that Mugabe was now going to be endorsed with no trouble at the party's annual conference in December. When the ZANU-PF annual conference took place on 17–19 December, Mugabe was not challenged for the position. In addition, the party endorsed his call for early elections in 2011. Mugabe had revealed that he was "tired" of the coalition deal and wanted an early poll so there could again be one man in charge of the government. As expected, ZANU-PF unanimously endorsed Mugabe as its presidential candidate. Not surprisingly, considering the threats and speculation following the release of the Wikileaks documents, the conference also passed a resolution "to call upon the Government to enforce the law of treason against any individual, corporate body or entity which calls for the imposition and or maintenance of sanctions or any other measures harmful, injurious and or deleterious to the welfare of the people of Zimbabwe".

On 11 October, it was reported that a ZANU-PF politburo member, Stanley Sakupwanya, and a former Manicaland governor and resident minister, Tineyi Chigudu, had defected to the revived *Zimbabwe African People's Union* (ZAPU). There were also reports that Cephas Msipa, the former governor and resident minister of the Midlands, had defected to ZAPU. On 29 August, former ZANU-PF politburo member Dumiso Dabengwa was unanimously endorsed as ZAPU president for the next five years at a congress reportedly attended by 5,000 delegates.

The smaller *MDC-M* also had its share of instability, disgruntlement and speculation. In early August, seven councillors in Bulilima in Matabeleland South defected to the mainstream MDC-T, citing that they "strongly [felt] the aims and founding values of the party [had] been compromised". Three more defections were reported in November. On 16 December, MDC-M leader Arthur Mutambara announced that he would not seek re-election at the party congress set for January 2011, amid reports that 11 out of 12 provinces had already indicated they would endorse Secretary-General Welshman Ncube as president. Mutambara cited purported divisions and disharmony among the party members over positions at the congress as influencing his decision not to seek re-election.

Zimbabwe's *controversial diamonds* were in the news all the year. On 3 March, it was announced that the South African Abbey Chikane, a founder chairman of the Kimberley Process (KP), had been appointed as the KP monitor for Zimbabwe. At its plenary in November 2009, the KP had agreed to implement a 12-step work programme to bring Zimbabwe into compliance with the KP Certification Scheme (KPCS). Under the plan, Zimbabwe had agreed to withhold any exports of diamonds from the notorious Marange diamond fields until prior approval by the monitor. In his report released in June, Chikane indicated that Zimbabwe had met the KP minimum requirements to sell its stockpiles of diamonds and recommended that Zimbabwe be allowed to export the stones. This prompted condemnations from human rights groups, who claimed that the military was still deeply involved in smuggling and violence against local miners. On 4 November, delegates from some 75 countries ended a four-day meeting in Jerusalem that had been deadlocked over whether to allow Zimbabwe to sell diamonds. Zimbabwe's reaction was to threaten to sell its diamonds with or without KP consent. On 23 November, Zimbabwe boycotted a KPSC meeting in Belgium.

The diamond controversy was not helped by the *arrest of a civil society activist.* On 3 June, Farai Maguwu, director of the Centre for Research and Development, who had been instrumental in exposing alleged human rights abuses in Zimbabwe's notorious Chiadzwa diamond fields, was arrested after turning himself in to police, following almost a week on the run from law enforcement and state security agents. A week before, his home and office had been raided by state security agents, who reportedly confiscated documents and equipment. The raid came just days after Maguwu had met with

Chikane. The arrest sparked outrage among international media, politicians and NGOs.

Foreign Affairs

As expected Zimbabwe maintained good relations with most *African countries* and organisations. Africa, and in particular SADC, continued its backing for the troubled GNU. As had become its custom, throughout the year, the MDC-T continued to refer unresolved matters about the GNU and GPA to SADC and the AU. Predictably, considering Africa's support for President Mugabe, the MDC-T strategy met with little success. Though there was a thaw in the country's relations with the West, this was not significant, as Zimbabwe's pariah status continued almost unchanged

As in previous years, *SADC*, especially under the chairmanship of South African President Jacob Zuma, the official SADC mediator for Zimbabwe, continued its efforts to prop up the GNU. Zuma visited Zimbabwe on 16 March to meet political parties on the implementation of the GPA. It was reported that Zuma would conduct an assessment of progress on the implementation of the GPA and see how SADC could assist in fast-tracking the processes. Zuma was in fact following his mediation team, which arrived in Zimbabwe on 15 March to meet the negotiators of the three parties ahead of their leader. On 16 June, it was reported that Zuma had again dispatched his facilitation team back to Zimbabwe to revive the stalled power sharing talks amid evidence of a fierce battle for the control of the GNU between Mugabe and Tsvangirai. Zuma dispatched yet another envoy (former transport minister Mac Maharaj) at the end of July in another attempt to kick-start the stalled talks. On 15 September, Tsvangirai and Zuma had a meeting in Johannesburg, which, according to Zuma's spokesperson, had been requested by the Zimbabwean prime minister. Tsvangirai wanted to push for the immediate implementation of the regional bloc's roadmap towards free and fair elections in 2011.

In August, it was reported that Zimbabwe was expected to hold *elections in 2011* using guidelines set up by SADC to ensure that a legitimate government was installed. The decision was made at a meeting of the SADC troika on defence and politics in Windhoek, Namibia, on 15 August. The troika resolved that, for Zimbabwe to progress, there had to be one leader properly elected through a free and fair election that produced credible results. The meeting was chaired by Mozambican President Armando Guebuza. It was attended by Zuma and the three principals to the GPA. SADC gave Zimbabwe a 30–day ultimatum. At the summit, Zuma said the parties to the GPA should resolve within a month outstanding issues threatening the GNU. The SADC leaders accepted and endorsed Zuma's recommendation.

Like SADC, the *AU*, a guarantor of the GPA, maintained its support of the GNU. It also called for sanctions to be removed. In July, Mugabe attended the AU Heads of State Summit in Kampala, Uganda. The only newsworthy item on Zimbabwe appeared to have been the fact that on 16 July, Mugabe collapsed on the stairs, fuelling frantic speculations about his health. On 4 August, the state media reported that Mugabe had gone to *Malawi* for closed-door talks with President Bingu wa Mutharika. There were wild rumours that he had gone for a traditional ceremony following the death of his sister, Sabina – a view that was unsurprisingly peddled by critics who insist that Mugabe was originally from Malawi.

Botswana maintained its critical stance on Zimbabwe. Deputy Permanent Secretary for Media Jeff Ramsay said in a 22 December press statement that SADC and the rest of the international community should insist on a process leading to credible elections in Zimbabwe. Obviously taking a dig at ZANU-PF's insistence that Mugabe was in charge, the statement asserted that no single party was ruling in Zimbabwe, but rather an inclusive government. The statement went on to point out that any decisions on an election date "must be arrived at by agreement of all parties and not through any unilateral pronouncements".

Notwithstanding SADC's public backing, there were moments of defiance on the part of Zimbabwe. On 26 January, High Court judge, Justice Bharat Patel, dismissed the 2008 ruling by the *SADC Tribunal* that declared the seizure of white-owned commercial farms unlawful. He said that the ruling by the Tribunal would have no effect in Zimbabwe, pointing out that he was "not entirely persuaded" that the Tribunal could "entertain and adjudicate alleged violations of human rights which might be committed by member states against their own nationals". According to Justice Patel, there was an "overwhelmingly negative impact of the Tribunal's decision on domestic law and agrarian reform in Zimbabwe, and notwithstanding the international obligations of the Government I am deeply satisfied that the registration and consequent enforcement of that judgment would be fundamentally contrary to the public policy of this country".

The issue of *'targeted sanctions'* dominated Zimbabwe's relations with the West. SADC consistently called for an end to sanctions on Zimbabwe. On 2 February, the EU renewed its sanctions against Zimbabwe for another 12 months, saying the unity government had not made enough progress. However, the EU lifted some sanctions while retaining 'targeted' sanctions on Mugabe and 142 senior ZANU-PF officials and business associates. Taken off the EU sanctions list were nine Zimbabwean companies and six individuals, including the ZAPU leader, Dumiso Dabengwa. On a state visit to the UK in March, President Zuma urged that sanctions should be eased to help Zimbabwe "move forward". Notably, on 5 October, Botswana's President Ian Khama, known for being critical of the ZANU-PF government, appealed for the first time to Western nations to lift sanctions on Zimbabwe, saying they should recognise the progress made by the GNU. However, on 4 March, the then British prime minister, Gordon Brown, said sanctions against Zimbabwe should not be lifted until human rights and media censorship concerns were addressed.

On 2 March, the *US* extended sanctions against Mugabe and his associates for another year. President Obama said that Zimbabwe's political crisis was still unresolved. In September, the US ruled out the lifting of sanctions imposed on Zimbabwe, accusing Mugabe's supporters of continuing human rights abuses and, on 21 December, imposed sanctions on Attorney General Tomana, a top Mugabe ally, for his alleged role in undermining democracy in Zimbabwe. The Treasury Department cited Tomana's targeting of selected political opponents, stating that it threatened the rule of law and the power-sharing deal. Like the US, other Western countries also maintained the sanctions.

President Mugabe maintained relations with leaders regarded as despots by Western democracies. On 22 April, the *Iranian President* Mahmoud Ahmadinejad began a state visit to Zimbabwe. Mugabe's opponents dismissed the visit as a meeting of despots which could further isolate Harare. Zimbabwean state media hailed Ahmadinejad's visit as part of a drive to strengthen ties between countries at odds with the West, but critics were quick to link the visit to Iran's nuclear programme and Zimbabwe's as yet unexploited uranium deposits.

Zimbabwe's relations with *China* remained strong. On 22 February, the Chinese embassy in Zimbabwe threw a birthday party for Mugabe and, on 26 February, Chinese Foreign Minister Yang Jiechi held talks in Beijing with visiting Zimbabwean Foreign Minister Simbarashe Mumbengegwi on bilateral relationship and international issues. On 19 April, at a luncheon she hosted for workers from China Jiangsu, the company that refurbished the National Sports Stadium, Vice President Joice Mujuru hailed the 'look east' policy, commended the Chinese government for its continued support for Zimbabwe and called for the strengthening of bilateral ties. On 31 May, a 25-strong Chinese Communist Party delegation led by Politburo member Wang Gang arrived in Zimbabwe. On 2 June at State House, cabinet members and the visiting delegation signed three bilateral agreements between Zimbabwe and China to strengthen economic ties. In August Mugabe visited China and, on 13 August, Chinese President Hu Jintao met with his Zimbabwean counterpart in the Great Hall of the People.

Zimbabwe's relations with *multilateral financial institutions* did not change very much. On 18 January, the AfDB announced that Zimbabwe would have to clear its arrears with international lending institutions before it could benefit from available funds. Notably, the AfDB disclosed that, at the time, it did not have a Country Strategy Paper for Zimbabwe and the country had not had Bank-funded project activity since 1999. On 19 February, the IMF announced that its Executive Board had decided to restore Zimbabwe's voting and related rights, and its eligibility to use resources from the IMF's General Resources Account (GRA), following a request from Zimbabwe's Finance Minister Tendai Biti. However, Zimbabwe would not be able to use resources from the GRA or the Poverty Reduction and Growth Trust (PRGT) until it fully settled its arrears of about $ 140 m to the PRGT. Since Zimbabwe had outstanding arrears owing to the PRGT, a number of remedial measures still remained in place, namely, the declaration of non-cooperation; the suspension of IMF technical assistance, except in targeted areas; and the removal of Zimbabwe from the list of PRGT-eligible countries. On 7 October, the World Bank Zimbabwe Manager Peter Nicholas said that the institution could not start funding major projects in Zimbabwe until the country cleared its $ 600 m debt, so the World Bank was not yet ready to fully re-engage Zimbabwe. Nichols announced that the Bank might provide nearly $ 3 m to help upgrade the country's failing water and sanitation infrastructure. These remarks came as Finance Minister Tendai Biti and Economic Planning Minister Tapiwa Mashakada were in Washington DC, meeting with officials from the US government and multilateral agencies to seek funding.

As usual, in September, Mugabe attended the *UN General Assembly* in New York. Apart from predictably condemning the "iniquitous sanctions" on Zimbabwe in his address on 24 September, he called for the democratisation of the UN and greater equality in international economic relations and decision-making structures.

Socioeconomic Developments

Key economic indicators showed that Zimbabwe's slow recovery continued. According to RBZ data, the all-items consumer price index increased marginally to 96.2%, up from 92.3% at the end of 2009. The year-on-year price increase rose to 3.3%, up from –7.7% the previous year. Significantly, deflation eased to 4.4% in January. Economist Intelligence Unit estimates put the nominal GDP at $ 1.6 bn, a slight improvement on $ 1.3 bn in 2009. International reserves increased to $ 152 m, while the debt service ratio declined marginally to $ 344 m from $ 351 m. According to the national budget statement (see below), economic growth was expected to increase to 8.1% in 2010 from 5.7% in 2009. Some $ 500 m of the budget was expected to be sourced from donor partners, most of whom had continued to withhold crucial aid.

On 25 November, Finance Minister Biti presented the *2011 budget* to parliament. It estimated the GDP at $ 5.5 bn. The current account deficit widened from $ 0.927 bn in 2009 to $ 1.041 bn due to increasing imports and non-factor services' receipts against lower exports. Notably, the budget acknowledged that transfers in 2010, such as remittances, declined, attributing this to "the effects of the global financial crisis". As at 31 October, the grand total of all external debt was $ 5.929 bn of which $ 4.769 bn were arrears. RBZ figures showed that central government remained the largest debtor with 57% of the debt, while parastatals and the private sector owed 35% and 8%, respectively. Total domestic budget revenues of $ 2.7 bn were projected for 2011 with anticipated external funding pushing the overall budget estimate to $ 3.2 bn. Of the proposed budget, $ 2.2 bn was applied towards recurrent expenditure.

As in the previous year, despite some decline in the downward slide, the public services, most notably *education and health* delivery systems, continued to experience problems of staffing, equipment and funding. As in recent years, health and educational personnel made up a substantial part of the brain drain to countries such as Australia, the UK, and South Africa. Industrial action and threats of industrial action arising out of salary disputes, particularly by doctors, nurses and teachers, were a constant feature, further compromising these sectors.

The *cholera epidemic* that had devastated the country the previous year declined by the beginning of the year, though there were still isolated cases. According to government figures released on 16 November by the National AIDS Council, the projected estimate for the adult *HIV prevalence* rate for the year was 13.7%. New HIV infections had decreased from nearly 66,000 the previous year to 61,000. Some observers argued that a rise in the number of people dying from AIDS had played a role in the decline, as well as an increase in the number of people (HIV positive or otherwise) who had migrated to other countries.

As in previous years, the poor economic situation led to multiple and complex *migration* issues, characterised by high levels of brain drain, cross border mobility and irregular migration. The net emigration rate was estimated at 12.7%.

Throughout the year, *electricity and water shortages* remained a problem, particularly in urban areas. Predictably, all these woes were explained in terms of 'illegal sanctions', a lack of foreign currency and sub-economic tariffs. On 8 January, it was reported that the Botswana Power Corporation and the Zimbabwe Electricity Supply Authority had signed an $ 8 m power deal that would see Botswana getting at least 40 MW from Zimbabwe. This was criticised by critics and businesses, which is not surprising, considering that Zimbabwe was itself experiencing huge power shortages.

Generally, the *food security* situation remained largely stable throughout the country, following improved harvests and the extension of the duty-free regulations to the end of the year. It was estimated that the majority of poor rural and urban households would be able to meet their minimum basic cereal requirements. However, changes were expected at the beginning of the October to December outlook period as cereal production stocks would diminish for a majority of the poor. According to the Zimbabwe Vulnerability Assessment Committee's rural livelihoods assessment in May, some 1.3 m rural people would not be able to meet their cereal requirements at the peak of the 2010/11 consumption year. Poor and very poor households in urban areas would probably remain vulnerable with limited income to buy food.

There was hope that Zimbabwe's troubled *diamond sector* would help alleviate the country's economic woes. However, the sector faced a lot of hiccups throughout the year (see above). On 7 January, a proposed 60,000 carats diamond auction was postponed, mainly due to uncertainty about the legality of the sale. On 11 August, Zimbabwe began a hugely controversial diamond auction with buyers from India, Israel, Russia, Lebanon and the US attending the auction. On 12 August, it was reported that the country had sold 900,000 carats of stockpiled diamonds worth more than $ 72 m. The government received 10% of the revenue as royalties.

The controversial *indigenisation and economic empowerment* policy was a divisive issue throughout the year, with mixed messages coming from government. On 9 February, the government gazetted the Indigenisation and Economic Empowerment (General) Regulations 2010 (Statutory Instrument 21 of 2010), which spelled out the country's indigenisation policy. They took effect on 1 March. The main objective of the regulations was to achieve 51% indigenous shareholding in existing businesses, with the owners given a five-year period to comply. The regulations stipulated that all existing businesses with a threshold of $ 500,000 should, within 45 days from 1 March, declare their shareholding status to the responsible minister through a prescribed form. New businesses would also be required to comply within 60 days. Throughout the year, the indigenisation and empowerment issue reflected the cracks within the GNU, with the MDC factions literally disowning the move and insisting it was not law, while ZANU-PF, and in particular Mugabe and his ministers, used it as a weapon of intimidation and a propaganda tool to win support. On 7 December, in a landmark policy climbdown the government announced it had shelved the legislation until "the local economy recovers".

Zimbabwe in 2011

Dominating the year was the love-hate relationship between the principals in the Government of National Unity (GNU) and mixed signals and disagreements over elections. Though the economy remained somewhat stable, there was persistent controversy over the Zimbabwe African National Union-Patriotic Front (ZANU-PF) indigenisation agenda and the Marange diamonds. Some political tensions persisted and incidents of political violence were reported. There was no major change on the foreign relations scene: the ZANU-PF part of the GNU continued to blame "illegal" sanctions for the country's woes, unrelentingly demanding their removal.

Domestic Politics

The year opened with President Robert Mugabe signalling his intentions to *call for elections*. On 23 January, he insisted that the GNU "was not meant to be a permanent arrangement". Stating that he had the constitutional power to call the elections even if electoral and constitutional reforms were not complete, Mugabe announced he would invoke those powers and call for elections during the year. Senior ZANU-PF politicians repeated the call. In May, Simon Khaya Moyo, the ZANU-PF national chairperson, told the Dutch ambassador that ZANU-PF's position was that the country had to conclude the constitution-making process and go to the polls. He asserted that the inclusive government had failed "because our policies with our colleagues in Government are different". In contrast, ZANU-PF's GNU partners were not so enthusiastic about elections. They insisted that the constitution-making process had to be finalised and outstanding issues in the Global Political Agreement (GPA) sorted out before credible elections could be held.

 | DOI:10.1163/9789004404335_005

The *constitution-making process* was mired in similar controversy. ZANU-PF officials wanted the Constitutional Parliamentary Committee (COPAC) to wrap up its work so that elections could be held. The body had insisted that the process could not be finished by year's end, and the projected completion time was March 2012. In October, COPAC announced that the referendum would not be held before February 2012, which meant that elections could not be held before mid-2012. ZANU-PF accused the Tsvangirai-led Movement for Democratic Change (MDC-T) of dragging out the process to postpone elections. On 21 April, negotiators from the three parties in the GNU announced that they had established a framework for holding future elections. It included the need for a new constitution to be in place before the elections, the lifting of sanctions and amendments to the Electoral Act. There was no agreement on security sector reforms as demanded by the MDC factions; nor was there agreement on having election observers in the country six months before elections, or on the demilitarisation of the Zimbabwe Electoral Commission.

There was a change of leadership in the *smaller faction of the MDC* led by Deputy Prime Minister Arthur Mutambara (MDC-M). On 8 January, Professor Welshman Ncube, the party's secretary general and GNU minister of industry and commerce, replaced Mutambara – who did not seek re-election – as party president. Henceforth the party was known as MDC-N. What started as a peaceful transition soon turned into an acrimonious power struggle between Mutambara and Ncube, each of whom had his own faction, and the Mutambara faction challenged the election of Ncube in the high court. On 8 February, Mutambara claimed he was still the MDC president and had fired Ncube. He (Mutambara) would remain president until the high court decided otherwise. The Ncube faction dismissed this and insisted that Ncube should replace Mutambara as deputy prime minister and GNU principal. However, Mutambara remained in post, thanks to Mugabe and Tsvangirai, who turned a deaf ear to requests by the Ncube faction. On 15 December, the high court dismissed Mutambara's challenge. The judge said Mutambara was not the legitimate leader of the party and could no longer 'purport' to be the party president. However, at year's end, Mutambara was still the deputy prime minister.

There was some activity on the *democracy and human rights* front. On 19 February, 45 members of the local chapter of the International Socialist Organisation (ISO) were arrested during an academic meeting where a video on the uprisings in Tunisia and Egypt was shown. Those arrested included Munyaradzi Gwisai, a former MDC legislator and president of the ISO. They were charged with treason and there were claims that the arrested activists were tortured in jail. On 28 February, the UN Special Rapporteur on Torture confirmed that he had written to the Zimbabwean government expressing concern about the torture allegations. On 19 July, the state prosecutor dropped the treason charges against the remaining six activists, who were finally indicted. The charges were downgraded to conspiracy to commit public violence, participating in a gathering with intent to promote public violence, or unlawfully acting together to endanger, promote or expose to hatred, contempt or ridicule the president and government.

Over the year, there were issues regarding *freedom of assembly*, with numerous MDC meetings being barred by the police. On 6 March, police barred most MDC restructuring meetings in Bulawayo, Midlands North, Mashonaland East and Mashonaland West. In Bulawayo, at least 20 police officers in full riot gear besieged the MDC provincial offices and ordered those attending the meeting to disperse, saying the meeting was illegal. On 4 April, police barred an MDC-T Kadoma Central district congress meeting, arguing that they had received orders from the Police General Headquarters in Harare to ban all MDC meetings in the district. Tsvangirai himself was barred from holding several rallies, including on 25 March, when he was prevented from holding a rally in Victoria Falls after police sealed the entrance to the stadium. Analysts took this as a sign of ZANU-PF's jitters over elections scheduled for 2012 and it was also seen as evidence of police partisanship, emphasising the need for security sector reform.

After a decline in 2010, political violence and human rights violations reportedly increased, with the parties blaming each other. Again, the security services and war veterans were fingered in quite a few of the incidents. There was widespread speculation that linked this *resurgence in violence* to the elections anticipated for 2012. On 29 May, Police Inspector Petros Mutedza was murdered outside a pub in the Harare township of Glen View, an MDC stronghold. Police quickly picked up 15 suspects, all members of the MDC-T, and the number soon swelled to 29. Those arrested included Solomon Madzore, the MDC-T Youth Assembly chairperson, who was arrested on 28 October. This again raised questions about the impartiality of the police, who had been accused of being an extension of ZANU-PF. The suspects were to spend the rest of the year in detention and the court was told that the suspects were tortured. On 6 November, there were violent clashes between ZANU-PF and MDC-T supporters in Chitungwiza, after the former stormed an MDC-T rally. On 7 November, Tsvangirai told journalists that the national executives of all three political parties in the GNU would meet on 11 November to discuss the worsening political violence in the country. ZANU-PF Central Committee members and their counterparts from the national executive councils of the MDC-T and MDC-N were expected to attend.

On 10 March, Energy and Power Development Minister Elton Mangoma (MDC-T) was arrested for criminal abuse of office in connection with a fuel deal he had made in December 2010. He was accused of by-passing tender procedures, spent more than a week in remand prison and was released after paying $ 5,000 bail. Some critics dismissed the arrest as a political ploy and as punishment for cutting ZANU-PF heavyweights from fuel deals. Signalling the *tension in the GNU*, Tsvangirai described Mangoma's arrest as a "calculated assault on the people of Zimbabwe". After a sensational high court trial, Mangoma was acquitted on 28 June. There was speculation that the arrest had been part of a broader plan by ZANU-PF to frustrate the GNU. On 18 April, MDC-T Treasurer-General Roy Bennett lost his senate seat after he had missed 21 consecutive sittings while exiled outside Zimbabwe. Bennett, who had been acquitted of treason charges, had left the country following threats that he would be arrested by the Joint Operations Command. All was not well within the GNU. In March, Tsvangirai claimed there were strong indications that Mugabe was no longer in charge of the country. On 27 March, the 'Daily News' quoted Tsvangirai as saying that many of the issues he agreed with Mugabe in their weekly meetings were often later reversed, ostensibly by security chiefs. He claimed that a 'coterie' of senior ZANU-PF officials was seemingly working full-time at undermining his efforts and working relationship with Mugabe. The 'coterie' was made up of senior people in the police, the military and the Central Intelligence Organisation, and included Defence Minister Emmerson Mnangagwa and Jonathan Moyo.

On 10 March, the Supreme Court nullified the election of Lovemore Moyo (MDC-T) as *speaker of the House of Assembly* on appeal. Four ZANU-PF legislators, including former information minister Jonathan Moyo, had challenged the MDC-T chairman's election in August 2008, claiming breaches of House rules on secret balloting. On 29 March, Moyo was re-elected, beating the ZANU-PF national chairman by 105 votes to 93. Earlier, on 21 March, MDC-N had indicated that its legislators would vote for the MDC-T candidate, claiming that ZANU-PF was planning to rig the election by reducing the numbers of MDC-T MPs through arrests. The voting suggested that at least two ZANU-PF MPs had voted for the MDC-T candidate. A witch-hunt followed within ZANU-PF, which saw a ZANU-PF legislator, Deputy Minister for Labour and Social Welfare Tracy Mutinhiri, being expelled from the party on 31 August for being a 'dissident'. She lost her ministerial post in December.

Throughout the year, there were numerous rumours about *Mugabe's purported illness* and failing health, which were mostly fiercely disputed by ZANU-PF. On 16 January, it was reported that Mugabe was in hospital in Malaysia after a prostate operation. On 13 February, presidential spokesman George Charamba announced that Mugabe had gone to Malaysia for eye checks. This was the only official acknowledgement of Mugabe's health problems. Stories of Mugabe's allegedly failing health surfaced again during the SADC summit in Zambia in April. There were further stories of trips to Singapore and Malaysia in October. On 2 October, Mugabe brushed aside reports that he was ill, saying he was in Singapore to rest and see his daughter, who was studying in Hong Kong.

On 15 August, retired *General Solomon Mujuru* died in a fire at his farm. Husband of Vice President Joice Mujuru and widely regarded as the ZANU-PF kingmaker, Mujuru was seen as the power behind one of the factions vying for control of ZANU-PF. There were numerous conspiracy theories about foul play, with some claims that it was an assassination. His death would have a huge impact on the succession issue and power struggles within ZANU-PF. A day after Mujuru's death, his wife, who was then the acting president, implored people to stop making wild statements on the cause of the death. On 20 October, the high court ordered an inquest.

The fallout from the release of diplomatic cables by the whistleblower website, *Wikileaks*, made further headlines. There was continued highlighting of reports of leading ZANU-PF politicians showing disenchantment with the party and Mugabe, mainly focussing on statements by some of his closest lieutenants saying he should retire. Also highlighted were claims that Mugabe had prostate cancer. The same reports also revealed that Tsvangirai had been criticised by his allies, quite a few of whom doubted his leadership credentials. There was speculation that Mugabe and Tsvangirai would act against the 'sell-outs', but no action was taken.

The *12th ZANU-PF Annual Conference* took place on 6–9 December in Bulawayo, with over 6,000 delegates attending. The most important resolutions were the widely anticipated (unopposed) nomination of Mugabe as party leader and an endorsement of the politburo decision that elections should be held in 2012, following which Mugabe would seek re-election. Other resolutions included the re-introduction of the Zimbabwe dollar and the call for NGOs to stay out of politics.

There were intermittent periods of *industrial unrest*, which mainly revolved around salaries of civil servants, dominated by teachers. On 19 January, public sector workers began an open-ended strike after wage talks collapsed, with Finance Minister Tendai Biti insisting there was no cash to meet the workers' demand. Unions affiliated to the umbrella body, the Apex Council, the main public sector union, were demanding a pay hike of 150%; the government had offered them 24%. The salary disputes were not resolved. In June, public sector workers again embarked on an indefinite strike to press the cash-strapped coalition government to more than double their wages. They wanted the lowest paid worker to take home around $ 500 per month. Civil servants were currently earning an average of $ 200 per month. In December, it was reported that a crippling civil service strike was looming in the New Year, again triggered by a groundswell of discontent over public sector remuneration packages. Unions gave the coalition government up to the end of December to have their salary concerns addressed or risk crippling strike action. ZANU-PF politicians and the pro-ZANU-PF media capitalised on the plight of workers to criticise the MDC-T, which was in charge of the labour and finance portfolios in the GNU.

Foreign Affairs

Although relations with most African and Asian countries and organisations remained largely friendly, there was little change in Zimbabwe's relations with the Western world. On a personal level, the MDC-T arm of the GNU had good relations with ZANU-PF's long-time Western critics. Sanctions, the GPA, Zimbabwe's debt, elections and indigenisation were some of the key issues that dominated foreign relations.

Relations with SADC – a guarantor of the GPA – were characterised by support and tensions with the regional body and with various member states. On 2 February, South Africa's President Jacob Zuma accepted Ambassador Phelekezela Mphoko's credentials as Zimbabwe's chief envoy to South Africa. Pro-ZANU-PF analysts saw this as a direct snub of an MDC-T request in 2010 for South Africa and other countries not to recognise ambassadors appointed by Mugabe. On 31 March, Zuma presented a damning report to the SADC troika meeting in Livingstone, Zambia, urging SADC to tighten the screws on ZANU-PF, since the situation in the country could no longer be tolerated and talk of polls was counter-productive. He warned that Zimbabwe could become another Egypt if there were no reforms. Following this report, the troika issued a communiqué calling for reform. The troika summit called for an end to violence and intimidation, the crafting of an electoral roadmap and the appointment of a SADC team to assist in the monitoring and evaluation of the GPA, among other things. This was an uncharacteristic censure of Mugabe and ZANU-PF and was interpreted by many as expressing the regional block's frustration with them.

On 3 April, the state-controlled weekly 'The Sunday Mail' published an *attack on Zuma*, labelling him "disaster prone". This spat resulted in tensions between the two countries, which were added to on 6 April by a piece in the state-controlled daily 'The Herald'. Mugabe's spokesperson distanced him from the attack on Zuma, pointing out that the stinging editorial was not the government view. South Africa's announcement that it would deport undocumented Zimbabweans residing in South Africa illegally (estimated to be more than a million) did nothing to improve relations between the two countries. Nevertheless, the ANC sent a delegation to ZANU-PF's annual conference and, on 8 December, ANC Secretary-General Gwede Mantashe pledged the ANC's support for ZANU-PF in the

Zimbabwean national elections, which were then expected to take place in 2012.

SADC *'facilitation'* continued throughout the year through a South African team appointed by Zuma. The team was led by Zuma's international advisor, Lindiwe Zulu, who became a target for attacks by the state controlled media because she often expressed critical views that were at odds with ZANU-PF's position. Some of the team's visits included meeting stakeholders beyond the three GNU parties. On 11 August, representatives from several civil society groups in Zimbabwe met with the facilitation team in Harare to present their positions on the electoral roadmap and other crucial issues, ahead of the 31st SADC summit in Luanda, Angola. On 13 December, the team reiterated that the SADC position on Zimbabwe was 'no reforms, no elections'. This was interpreted as meaning that there would be no elections in 2012. On 19 May, the special SADC summit in Windhoek, Namibia, did not have Zimbabwe on the agenda. The 31st ordinary session of SADC in Angola was significant in that Tsvangirai was not invited as prime minister, but attended as an ordinary citizen. NGO activists from Zimbabwe were also barred from the summit, and Zimbabwe was not on the agenda. The Extraordinary Summit of SADC Heads of State and Government was held in Johannesburg, South Africa, on 11–13 June. There was disagreement as to whether the summit adopted the resolution of the Livingstone troika and Zuma's scathing report. While the MDC factions and their allies insisted it did, ZANU-PF-aligned analysts and politicians insisted it did not, but had simply 'noted' it. The communiqué and the statements of the facilitators, however, indicated they did indeed adopt it, which was seen as a blow to Mugabe and ZANU-PF.

On 27 January, Mugabe arrived in Addis Ababa, Ethiopia, to attend the 16th Ordinary Session of the *AU General Assembly*. Despite attempts by activists to drag Zimbabwe onto the AU agenda, there was no condemnation of Mugabe and ZANU-PF. Analysts interpreted this as a result of the AU's preoccupation with urgent issues, among them the unrest in North Africa and Côte d'Ivoire.

At an official level, there was hardly any thaw in *relations with the West*. Mugabe and ZANU-PF officials continued to blame Zimbabwe's woes on "illegal" Western sanctions. This was not helped by the continuation and/or renewal of targeted sanctions by the EU, USA and Australia, among others. In March, Mugabe launched an ambitious campaign to get two million signatures on an "anti-sanctions petition" calling for the unconditional lifting of all measures imposed by the West. On 15 February, the EU announced the extension of sanctions, but removed 35 people from the list of sanctions targets. This left 163 individuals and 31 businesses on the list for 'restrictive measures'. Unsurprisingly, while noting significant progress in addressing Zimbabwe's economic crisis and in the delivery of basic social services, the EU expressed deep concern about political violence. On 9 March, the USA extended by another year its sanctions regime targeting Mugabe and top ZANU-PF officials, citing lack of progress on political reform and continuing human rights abuses. The West was also seen as frustrating Zimbabwe's attempts to sell its diamonds legally. While most developing countries supported the move, Western countries remained opposed. On 12 December, the USA imposed sanctions on two diamond mines located in Zimbabwe's Marange region, the scene of alleged serious human rights abuses in 2008. A mine belonging to state-owned Marange Resources and another owned by Mbada Diamonds were added to a US Treasury Department list targeting entities' linked to ZANU-PF. At its meeting in Kinshasa on 1 November, the Kimberley Process Certification Scheme cleared Zimbabwe to resume the supervised export of diamonds from its troubled Marange field. The deal was brokered by the EU. In June, it was reported that the country had exported diamonds worth $ 90 m between January and April, despite the ban on sales.

Good relations with traditional *allies in the east* continued, with China and Iran being particularly close. On 1 February, ministers claimed that Zimbabwe was in line for a windfall of up to $ 10 bn from China, a potentially huge boost to the ailing economy. The

GNU presented a united front on the issue, with even MDC-T ministers insisting that Chinese investment in mining and agriculture could help turn the economy around. On 21 March, Zimbabwe and China signed a raft of agreements worth $ 585 m through the Chinese Development Bank, aimed at reviving the health, mining and agricultural sectors. The signing ceremony was attended by Chinese Vice Premier Wang Qishan, who was in Zimbabwe on an official visit. He pledged support for Zimbabwe's economic recovery and promised to lobby for the lifting of Western sanctions. On 17 November, Mugabe, who was visiting China, held talks with Vice President Xi Jinping in Beijing. Xi Jinping described Mugabe as "a famed leader of the national liberation movement in Africa".

On 6 March, a leaked intelligence report compiled by the International Atomic Energy Agency, the UN nuclear watchdog, suggested *Iran* would be awarded exclusive access to Zimbabwe's *uranium* in return for providing the country with fuel. Zimbabwe's uranium stocks consisted of an estimated 455,000 tonnes at Kanyemba, north of Harare. The report revealed that Iran's foreign and co-operative ministers had visited Zimbabwe to strike the deal, and sent engineers to assess uranium deposits. On 8 March, the USA warned Zimbabwe that it could face international penalties if it helped Iran's nuclear programme in defiance of UN sanctions and a global arms treaty.

Relations with *multilateral financial institutions* were mixed. In March, the AfDB reopened its Zimbabwe office after a ten-year absence, citing an improved political climate, and, on 7 March, announced a $ 51.55 m injection into a fund to aid the economy. The regional lender had left Zimbabwe in 2000 due to a breakdown in its relationship with the government and Zimbabwe's failure to service its external debt. On 10 June, the AfDB and the Zimbabwean government signed a $ 30 m grant agreement in support of the urgent water supply and sanitation rehabilitation project. In June, the IMF said Zimbabwe's economic outlook for 2011 was uncertain, and warned of a "sizeable" fiscal financing gap and uncertainty over the country's business climate. In the statement following the conclusion of Article IV consultations, the IMF executive board applauded the positive economic changes that had occurred since the formation of the GNU, including a 9% increase in real GDP in 2010. The board said, however, that several factors mitigated against similar growth for 2011, noting that the existing policy environment and the controversial indigenisation programme would deter economic expansion. The growth forecast was downgraded from 7% to 5.5%.

Socioeconomic Developments

There were some continued improvements in *key economic indicators*. Reserve Bank of Zimbabwe figures showed that the consumer price index closed the year at about 100%. Economist Intelligence Unit estimates put the nominal GDP at $ 2 bn, up from $ 1.6 bn in 2010. The official budget estimated the 2011 GDP at $ 8.073 bn, indicating a GDP growth of 9.3%. The current account balance, excluding transfers, improved from –$ 1,041.1 m in 2010 to –$ 58.6 m in 2011. In the budget statement, the finance minister put the external debt at $ 6.9 bn, of which $ 4.8 bn were arrears.

In February, it was reported that there were more than 75,000 *ghost workers in the civil service* out of a total of 180,000 public servants employed. Most of these were said to be unqualified ZANU-PF militia members and supporters. The ghost workers were unearthed by a comprehensive payroll and skills audit done by Ernst & Young (India) on behalf of the ministry of public service. The issue was quickly politicised when the Public Service Commission disputed the findings, producing its own figures to prove its argument about the non-existence of ghost workers. ZANU-PF characteristically claimed that the audit had been hijacked by a British employee in the prime minister's office. The scandal lent weight to claims that the civil service had become a haven for ZANU-PF patronage.

On 25 March, Minister of Youth Development, Indigenisation and Empowerment Saviour Kasukuwere gazetted the *Indigenisation and Economic Empowerment Regulations*. The regulations set out key amendments to the implementation of the indigenisation and empowerment programme in mining companies not controlled by indigenous Zimbabweans. The regulations significantly altered the minimum threshold by requiring that the disposal of 51% of the shares in non-indigenous mining companies to designated entities would apply to all companies with a net asset value of more than $ 1 rather than the $ 500,000 threshold stipulated in the 2010 regulations. This drastically widened the scope of the indigenisation programme to encompass all non-indigenous mining companies operating in Zimbabwe. The timeframe for compliance was shortened to six months from the date of publication of the regulations. In addition, the new regulations required that affected non-indigenous companies submit an indigenisation implementation plan by 9 May. Some companies, notably the South African-owned Implants, started facing pressure from empowerment groups, including traditional leaders who were demanding a 10% stake in the company. While ZANU-PF and its allies backed the regulations, industry and the MDC-T expressed concern about their effect on investment. There were reports that the Chamber of Mines had taken legal advice on the legality and practicality of the regulations, indicating that there were possible grounds for appeal.

On 20 April, the government launched the draft *Industrial Development Policy* covering the period 2011–2015, aimed at reviving four key sectors of the economy: agro-processing, the fertiliser industry, pharmaceuticals, and metals and electricals. The policy sought to increase the manufacturing sector's contribution to GDP to 20% from the current 12%, and to increase the contribution of exports from the sector from 26% of GDP to 50% by 2015. On 27 September, the cabinet adopted the policy. On 7 July, the coalition government launched the *Medium Term Plan* (MTP) 2011–2015. The MTP was expected to pave the way for various policies and programmes addressing the macro-economic fundamentals critical for the growth of the economy.

Throughout the year, Zimbabwe's *underperforming parastatals* experienced various problems. Leading in news coverage were the national carrier Air Zimbabwe, integrated steel manufacture Ziscosteel, and the power utility Zimbabwe Electricity Supply Authority (ZESA). There were issues about debt, mismanagement and corruption. In May, the Civil Aviation Authority of Zimbabwe declared Air Zimbabwe's three planes (all Boeing 737s) a public danger, having reached the limit of 34,000 cycles. On 18 May, Air Zimbabwe cancelled all domestic and regional flights, leaving hundreds of travellers stranded. On 4 March, ZESA's CEO announced that the power utility was technically bankrupt. ZESA's debts had mounted to $ 889 m and its liabilities exceeded its assets. ZESA was failing to meet the country's power supply requirements, with national demand of 2,100 MW outstripping internal generation of about 1,200 MW. On 9 March, Industry and Commerce Minister Welshman Ncube described the country's sole integrated steel manufacturing company, Ziscosteel, as "insolvent, valueless and in a state of disrepair". Ncube was responding to questions from the media after the signing of a deal that saw the Indian firm Essar Africa Group take control of the company. The Indian-based company, through Essar Africa Holdings Ltd, had bought a 54% stake in the ailing debt-ridden state-owned steelmaker. The total deal value was $ 750 m, of which $ 340 m was debt.

About 1.7 m people were estimated to have no *food security* during the peak lean season from October through February. About 400,000 of the food insecure people were estimated to be in urban areas, and those in the rural areas outside of the central districts were classified to be moderately food insecure. Food assistance programme plans for the period of January through to March were deemed to be sufficient to cover the assessed needs. According to Reliefweb, food imports would continue to be a significant component of Zimbabwe's food supply in the outlook period. Since many Zimbabweans still relied on markets for their basic needs, global food and fuel price trends were likely to impact the purchasing power for very poor and poor households. Another worrying development was the poor rainfall season experienced in the southern districts of Masvingo and Matabeleland South provinces. It was estimated that the summer harvest would be substantially lower even than the previous year. In the second half of the year, food security remained generally stable at the national level, with staple cereals and basic food stuffs readily available on the market. Own staple cereal production and purchases were the main sources for most households in both urban and rural areas.

In August, it was reported that the *humanitarian situation* in the country still remained fragile, with food security, health, water and sanitation a serious cause for concern. Millions of people were said to be drinking from unprotected water sources and living in unhygienic conditions. Due to the immediate humanitarian needs, aid agencies appealed through the UN Office for the Coordination of Humanitarian Affairs for $ 488 m, an increase of $ 73 m from the original requirements of $ 415 m. Key priorities to be addressed by the revised 2011 Consolidated Appeal Process included improving levels of food security, which had been described as a "pressing issue", nutrition, water and sanitation, and addressing the needs of asylum seekers and other vulnerable groups. About 4.95 m women and children were in need of immediate nutritional facilities.

On 24 November, Finance Minister Tendai Biti presented his *2012 national budget*. He proposed a $ 4 bn budget, with resumed trading in the country's diamond resources expected to contribute an additional $ 600 m. He further projected a growth rate of 9.4% for 2012, with agriculture and mining as the major drivers. The budget revised the tax-free threshold from the $ 225 for 2011 to $ 250, starting on 1 January 2012. One of the major highlights of the budget was the envisaged creation of the three-year rolling finance strategy for the agricultural sector.

Despite some marked improvements, the *education and health* delivery systems continued to experience problems of staffing, equipment and funding. Health and educational personnel remained a substantial part of the brain drain to countries such as Australia, the United Kingdom, and South Africa. Industrial action and threats of industrial action arising out of salary disputes, particularly by doctors, nurses and teachers, were a constant feature throughout the year, further compromising these sectors.

Zimbabwe continued to lose skilled manpower, through *migration*, mainly to Commonwealth countries. According to the World Bank, emigrants from Zimbabwe in 2010 were estimated to number 1,253,100, which amounted to about 10% of the population. The net emigration rate was estimated at 24.83 per 1,000 of the population. Top destination countries were South Africa, the United Kingdom, Mozambique, Australia, Zambia, the United States, Malawi, New Zealand, Canada and Ireland. The situation of Zimbabwean migrants in South Africa remained precarious, with threats of deportation of undocumented migrants looming. Attempts by the government to issue documents to Zimbabweans in South Africa did not remove the threat, as many remained undocumented. In March, thousands of failed Zimbabwean asylum-seekers in the UK faced deportation after asylum judges ruled there was no evidence that those being returned would generally be at risk of harm. The UK Border Agency promptly announced that Britain would resume the forcible return of Zimbabweans whose asylum claims had been rejected. More than 10,000 Zimbabwean failed asylum-seekers were believed to be in Britain, of whom some 3,000 had exhausted all avenues of appeal. The move was strongly resisted by human rights groups, which continued to warn of harassment and persecution of opponents of ZANU-PF.

In November, there was an outbreak of *typhoid* in the densely populated residential areas of Harare, attributed to a lack of clean water and adequate sanitation in the townships. Most of the typhoid infections occurred in the over-crowded township of Dzivaresekwa, where untreated sewage flowed in the streets. Experts warned it might herald the resurgence of cholera, but this did not materialise. According to government figures, the adult *HIV* prevalence was 14.3% in 2010. It is not yet known whether the downward trend is a sign of long-term change or merely a temporary respite. The charity Avert warned that, given the large number of homeless and displaced people living in Zimbabwe who were not likely to have been surveyed, the results could not be taken as wholly representative of the situation. In November, there were reports of an acute shortage of drugs for anti-retroviral therapy (ART) in Beitbridge District, where around 20,553 people were in need of life-prolonging drugs. Only 20% of patients with HIV had been placed on ART due to limited resources. The situation was not different in many parts of the country.

Zimbabwe in 2012

The year was characterised by an escalation of disagreements and interparty squabbling over the constitution and elections dates. The love-hate relationship between the coalition partners in the Government of National Unity (GNU) continued. There were some controversies and notable developments in human rights, indigenisation and the security sector reforms. The economy remained stable with the post GNU improvements appearing to be moderating amid occasional scare-mongering about the state of the national finances and persistent disagreements over the direction of economic and monitory policy. No significant changes took place on the international scene, either regionally or beyond.

Domestic Politics

The country moved closer to getting a new constitution. On 22 January, the three drafters handed the revised copy of the *draft constitution* to the co-chairpersons of the Constitutional Parliamentary Committee (COPAC). On 9 February, COPAC released a press statement signed by all three party co-chairpersons. It stressed that the draft, described as "work in progress until it is approved by COPAC" was not final and was still under review by the Select Committee assisted by technical experts. On 7 March, COPAC announced that the co-chairpersons and technical experts had completed reviewing the draft and were ready to hand it to the management committee within the week. Reflecting the acrimony that had characterised the process and was to continue with the draft, the state-controlled, openly pro-Zimbabwe African National Union-Patriotic Front (ZANU-PF) daily 'The Herald', reported on 7 March that COPAC had "made a raft of changes ... after principal drafters inserted information not solicited from the people". The paper probably reflected ZANU-PF's

 | DOI:10.1163/9789004404335_006

mistrust of the technical experts, who the party had persistently argued were biased against the party.

Deep *divisions between the main political parties* on various aspects of the draft constitution persisted throughout the year. A particularly contentious issue was the degree of regionalisation and devolution. The Movement for Democratic Change (MDC) factions favoured devolution whereas ZANU-PF was strongly opposed to the concept, opting for much less radical decentralisation. Outside the main political parties, there was criticism by civil society organisations. Many of them complained about the retention of the features of a strong executive presidency. In addition to retaining the powers to dissolve parliament, in the draft, the president still remained the head of state and government and commander-in-chief of the defence forces. There was no limit to the number of ministers, and parliament was enlarged to 270 members in a two-tier system. Other contentious issues included dual citizenship and homosexuality, with ZANU-PF predictably being against both, while the Tsvangirai-led party (MDC-T) was in favour of enshrining legal protection for them in the constitution. On 6 June, ZANU-PF walked out of a COPAC meeting when a highly controversial document containing their input and amendments to the draft was rejected. The MDC formations stood by the COPAC draft. Speculation was rife that ZANU-PF was raising all manner of petty objections in order to scuttle the new constitution because the party wanted elections held under the existing constitution, which gave them an advantage. On 22–23 October, COPAC's *Second All Stakeholders' Conference* to discuss the proposed new constitution took place in Harare and was attended by 1,300 delegates from the country's ten provinces. In a rare moment of agreement, representatives of the three GNU parties proclaimed the conference a success, publicly indicating that they were happy with the deliberations.

Throughout the year the coalition partners publicly disagreed about dates for the *next elections.* Whereas the MDC formations maintained that elections did not necessarily have to be held when the life of the current parliament expired in May 2013, ZANU-PF disagreed, insisting that elections should be held in March 2013. The MDC factions had the backing of South Africa's President Jacob Zuma, the SADC chief facilitator on Zimbabwe. Together they insisted that, in addition to an agreed constitution, other electoral measures needed to be in place before credible elections could be held. On 12 July, the Supreme Court confirmed a High Court order that President Mugabe should call *by-elections* in three Matabeleland constituencies by the end of August. In court papers asking for an extension, Mugabe revealed on 27 September that he wanted to hold elections in March 2013, with a referendum on a new constitution taking place in November 2012. Not surprisingly, the MDC-T dismissed this as unrealistic. On 11 October, in an interview with the BBC, Justice Minister Patrick Chinamasa, the ZANU-PF negotiator under the Global Political Agreement (GPA) talks, echoed the position of senior military officials that ZANU-PF and the military would not accept an MDC-T election victory, since such a victory would have been imposed by foreign powers. On 20 October, MDC-T Secretary-General and GNU Finance Minister Tendai Biti called for the arrest of Chinamasa and ZANU-PF spokesperson, Rugare Gumbo, who had made similar remarks, accusing them of plotting to subvert the will of the people in the forthcoming elections. Gumbo had warned on 18 October that it would be "messy" if Tsvangirai won the elections. This was interpreted as a threat of a bloodbath in the event of an MDC-T electoral victory.

Controversy persisted regarding *human rights, democracy and the rule of law*. The police featured prominently in these developments, with complaints continuing throughout the year that they were a partial force serving ZANU-PF. Notably, on 9 October, Energy and Power Development Minister Elton Mangoma was arrested for allegedly insulting Mugabe at a rally in March. On 12 March, the trial of 29 MDC-T activists accused of murdering a police officer, Inspector Petros Mutedza, in May 2011, began at the High Court. The MDC-T and other critics of ZANU-PF saw this as political victimisation, maintaining that it showed the partiality of the police and the office of the attorney general. They interpreted it as persecution by prosecution. The 29 activists, who had spent more than a year in jail, were repeatedly denied bail. According to opponents of the regime, this reflected that the judiciary was not impartial. On 17 December, 21 of the accused were finally granted bail, leaving five still incarcerated. Three others had been released earlier in the year.

During the year, the police issued numerous *bans on MDC meetings* in various parts of the country. On 23 April, police arrested 15 activists of the smaller MDC in Tsholotsho South in Matabeleland North province for conducting an 'illegal' meeting. On 14 August, police in Bulawayo banned a memorial service for MDC activist Patrick Nabayana. He had disappeared in 2000 and it was believed that he had been murdered. In August, Mashonaland West police wrote to the MDC-T provincial leadership, advising the party that no meetings would be held without the authority of chiefs, headmen, kraal heads and councillors – most of them widely viewed as ZANU-PF apparatchiks. The MDC-T vowed to defy the directive. During the year, there was an upsurge in the number of people arrested for allegedly *insulting President Mugabe*. The human rights organisation Zimbabwe Lawyers for Human Rights reportedly represented over 50 individuals who were dragged to court for calling Mugabe all sorts of names. Those arrested included ordinary people, businesspeople and MDC officials. The upsurge in arrests was partly attributed to the overzealousness of police and security agents.

Factionalism, intra-party fighting and tensions affected all three major political parties. In July, the ZANU-PF politburo directed that all District Coordination Committees (DCCs) be disbanded. Most of the DCCs were seen as being controlled by the faction aligned to Defence Minister Emmerson Mnangagwa. Their dissolution was therefore interpreted as a blow to the faction. The faction aligned to Vice President Joice Mujuru was seen as the main beneficiary of the controversial directive, and was widely thought to have orchestrated the move. Explaining the decision, Mugabe said the DCCs were "serving a divisive process" and hence "as an organ they must go". Infighting in the MDC-T was also reported in a number of provinces, including Bulawayo and the Midlands. In August, MDC-T Secretary for Local Government Sessil Zvidzai was fingered in the dismissal of the mayor and six other councillors as part of preparations to grab the Gweru Urban seat. Zvidzai justified their dismissal as part of the party's anti-corruption drive. MDC-T's Bulawayo province was also rocked by factionalism. On 13 July, MDC-T supporters in Makokoba, Bulawayo, demonstrated against worsening factionalism in the party's Bulawayo structures, which had reportedly resulted in a number of defections. Splits and clashes rocked the party in Masvingo, Manicaland and Mashonaland East. The smaller faction of the MDC, which itself had split into two factions, continued divided with faction leaders, Deputy Prime Minister Arthur Mutambara and Industry and Commerce Minister Welshman Ncube, fighting for the coveted role of principal in the GPA. On 12 July, the High Court ruled in favour of Ncube as the legitimate leader of the MDC faction. Mutambara appealed to the Supreme Court. The High Court decision was widely interpreted as putting Mutambara's position as the country's deputy prime minister in jeopardy. However, throughout the year, Mugabe and Tsvangirai, the other principals, continued to deal with Mutambara, ignoring Ncube's pleas to remove him. In August, the SADC summit resolved that Ncube was the recognised MDC principal, even though the party leadership dispute was still pending in the Supreme Court.

Politically motivated violence, though not at the pre-GNU levels, was reported in parts of the country. On 31 March, the Zimbabwe Peace Project (ZPP), a violence-monitoring group, reported an upswing in violence in the previous month. It linked this to Mugabe's insistence that he would call elections in 2012. ZPP reported 413 cases of rights violations in February alone, which occurred in connection with ZANU-PF's preparation of the forthcoming elections. Teachers continued to be among the worst affected by violence. On 28 November, the Zimbabwe Human Rights NGO Forum (Zimrights) reported that, for over a year, notorious war veteran leader Jabulani Sibanda had camped in Masvingo Province. He terrorised civil servants, traditional leaders and villagers and conducted rallies and meetings disguised as history lessons. Echoing concerns about selective law enforcement and prosecution, Zimrights blamed the escalation on a culture of impunity in which ZANU-PF members were not brought to justice. Notably, during the year, Mugabe made numerous calls for peace and peaceful elections, which critics and opponents dismissed as insincere.

Persistent *rumours* about Mugabe's purported illness and failing health continued. Predictably, ZANU-PF and the presidency rejected the rumours. The most sensational claims were contained in the British press on 9 April, where it was reported that a cancer-stricken Mugabe was fighting for his life in a Singapore hospital. On 10 April, ZANU-PF dismissed the reports as "a lot of hogwash" and the rumours proved to be untrue. The love life and alleged promiscuity of the widowed MDC-T leader Morgan Tsvangirai were in the news for a good part of the year. Tsvangirai was linked to no less than four women and allegedly had a child with one of them. ZANU-PF and the state-controlled press capitalised on these escapades, constantly raising questions about Tsvangirai's suitability as a leader and role model.

The 13th annual *ZANU-PF conference* took place on 7–10 December in Gweru, in a $ 6.2 m complex built specially for the conference by a Chinese company. Among the conference's notable resolutions was the confirmation of Mugabe, formerly elected at the previous congress, as the party's presidential candidate in the harmonised elections to be held in 2013; the backing of indigenisation and economic empowerment; and spearheading the adoption of currencies of the BRICS (Brazil-Russia-India-China-South Africa) countries and other emerging economies as legal tender in Zimbabwe alongside the US dollar.

Save for minor strikes and incessant threats of strikes for higher wages, there was some let-up in *industrial unrest*. On 19 January, civil servants went on a one-day strike, but it was reportedly not well supported. On 21 January, the MDC-T accused ZANU-PF of encouraging civil servants to strike in order to gain political mileage. This came after civil servants had warned that government operations, including offices, schools and hospitals, would come to a standstill as they embarked on a one-week strike to press for better salaries. On 5 July, civil servants gave government a two-week ultimatum to review salaries or face a strike. On 24 July, it was reported that just 100 civil servants in Harare went on a protest march to denounce the government's failure to meet their salary demands.

Foreign Affairs

As in previous years, relations with most African and Asian countries and organisations remained largely friendly. The frosty relations with the traditional Western critics changed little, with ZANU-PF escalating its campaign against 'illegal' Western sanctions. Not surprisingly the 'illegal' *sanctions* dominated the foreign relations scene.

SADC, as the guarantor of the GPA, continued its mediation efforts, as individual countries mostly supported the GNU or parts of it. Notable in this respect was Zambian President Michael Sata's strident support for Mugabe and ZANU-PF. On 24 January, in an interview with the UK 'Telegraph', Sata labelled Tsvangirai a "western stooge", indicating that he would not block Mugabe's push to abandon the unity government. At a SADC extraordinary summit held in Luanda (Angola) on 1 June, Sata kept chanting pro-ZANU-PF slogans, interrupting anyone who criticised Mugabe. Relations between Mugabe and his Botswana counterpart Ian Khama appeared to be thawing. On 23 May, in what was dubbed a 'secret visit', second vice president John Nkomo arrived in Gaborone (Botswana) leading an 11-member delegation and held a brief meeting with Khama. Mugabe also dispatched his defence and state security ministers with special messages to the leaders of Angola and Zambia in what was interpreted as a campaign to seek regional backing for elections in 2012. SADC was again called upon to intervene in the squabbling over *elections*. On 1 June, at the Extraordinary Summit of SADC Heads of State and Government in Luanda, the regional body effectively ended Mugabe's plans to hold polls during the year without any meaningful reforms. In its communiqué, SADC "urged the parties to the GPA to finalise the constitution-making process and subject it to a referendum thereafter". The summit also urged the parties to the GPA, assisted by President Zuma, to develop an implementation mechanism and to set out time frames for the full implementation of the roadmap to elections. Both the MDC-T and ZANU-PF interpreted this as a vindication of their positions. On 18 August, a full SADC summit in Maputo (Mozambique) affirmed these resolutions, again urging "the parties to the GPA to develop a roadmap together with timelines that are guided by requirements of the processes necessary for the adoption of the constitution of conditions for free and fair elections to be held". Notably, this summit recognised Welshman Ncube, the MDC-N leader, as a GPA principal. On 8 December, the SADC summit in Dar es Salaam (Tanzania) again urged the political stakeholders in Zimbabwe to fully implement the GPA, and called on the political stakeholders to finalise the constitutional process – including a referendum – before the holding of elections in 2013. As expected, the parties gave their own political spin to the communiqué, declaring victory for their own positions.

President Zuma's *facilitation of the GPA* continued to generate controversy, with ZANU-PF becoming hostile and MDC-T referring quite a few GPA disputes to Zuma. This saw an increase in the number of visits to Harare by Zuma's facilitation team. On 28 May, a strong facilitation team, comprising senior figures Lindiwe Zulu, Mac Maharaj and Charles Nqakula, was in Harare for talks with the negotiators of the three GPA parties. On 28 August, the team held a meeting with GPA negotiators in Harare on attempts to revive the stalled constitutional reform process. The visit followed a weekend decision by ZANU-PF's politburo that their amended draft charter was "final and non-negotiable", while the MDC formations insisted that the agreed version be taken to the All Stakeholders Conference. On 8 October, the team visited Harare for briefings on progress with the finalisation of a new constitution, which had become a condition for the holding of elections. On 27 November, a two-member facilitation team arrived in Harare for two-day talks with the three GPA parties, where they were told of lack of progress. Senior ZANU-PF officials became increasingly critical of Zuma's facilitation. In a scathing attack in an online newspaper on 19 August, Jonathan Moyo described Zuma as "troubled" and accused him of unilaterally installing Ncube as GPA principal. ZANU-PF apparently supported Julius Malema in his fight against Zuma. These attacks did not, however, seem to change ZANU-PF's relationship with Zuma, the ANC and the South African government. On several occasions during the year, South Africa called for the lifting of sanctions against Zimbabwe. In a statement on 29 August, the MDC formation led by Deputy Prime Minister Arthur Mutambara attacked what it described as "the persistent and pestering attitude of the Zuma facilitation team". This was probably a response to Zuma's purported influence in having SADC make decisions that did not support the positions of ZANU-PF and Mutambara's MDC faction.

Relations with the EU remained frosty. On 17 February, the EU announced that 'restrictive measures' against Zimbabwe should be renewed until 20 February 2013. On the list were 112 individuals and 11 entities. Ostensibly to facilitate further dialogue between the EU and the government of Zimbabwe, the travel ban imposed on the two members of the 're-engagement team', Justice Minister Patrick Chinamasa and Foreign Minister Simbarashe Mumbengegwi, were lifted. On 22 March, the EU renewed its 'restrictive measures' against rough diamonds from Zimbabwe's Marange area until February 2013. On 23 May, Attorney General Johannes Tomana filed a lawsuit against the EU, seeking the removal of sanctions targeting Mugabe and his close allies, claiming that the measures were illegal and violated their rights.

There was no improvement in relations with the *USA*. In January, the USA imposed sanctions on two state-owned diamond-mining companies, although this was unlikely to affect sales of Zimbabwean stones to destinations such as India and Dubai. Finance Minister Tendai Biti attacked the US government for imposing the ban. In May, the US Assistant Secretary for African Affairs Johnnie Carson vowed that the USA would not lift sanctions imposed on Mugabe and many top officials before there were signs of permanent political reforms. On 14 November, a US diplomat said sanctions on Zimbabwe would remain until the human rights situation improved.

Relations with multilateral organisations were mixed. In May, *UN High Commissioner for Human Rights* Navi Pillay visited Zimbabwe, calling on 25 May for the suspension of targeted international sanctions pending the holding of elections. Expressing views that resonated with ZANU-PF's stance on sanctions, she claimed that the measures were hurting the country's poorest and most vulnerable people. In June, an *IMF* team visited Zimbabwe for routine Article IV consultations. The subsequent report reflected the usual worries about, among other things, Zimbabwe's arrears on external payments. In a statement issued on 30 October, the IMF announced that it had relaxed most restrictions on technical assistance to Zimbabwe. This opened the way for future staff-monitored programmes and full normalisation of relations. The IMF executive board would also resume IMF technical assistance in new areas to support the country's formulation and implementation of a comprehensive adjustment and structural reform programme to be monitored by its staff. In a major endorsement, on 27 July the *World Bank* described Zimbabwe's plans to settle $ 10.7 bn of foreign debt as "reasonable". Mugabe's criticism of the *UNSC* continued unabated. In a speech before the UN General Assembly on 26 September, he said the UNSC had allowed itself to be "abused" by authorising the use of force in Libya.

Good relations with traditional allies in the east continued, and were particularly close with China and Iran. In October, the Iran-

Zimbabwe Joint Commission was inaugurated in Tehran (Iran). Meetings took place between the respective foreign ministers. *Iran* expressed satisfaction with the level of Tehran-Harare cooperation. In March, there were sensational reports that Zimbabwe's role as a potential conduit for military equipment destined for Iran was likely to come under the spotlight as international agencies probed claims that bribes were solicited in South Africa for sanctions-busting deals with Iran. The reports came as Iranian President Mahmoud Ahmadinejad was meeting Defence Minister Emmerson Mnangagwa in Tehran. At a meeting between Mnangagwa and Iranian Defence Minister Ahmad Vahidi, Iran pledged to help Zimbabwe to modernise its defence forces. Some critics interpreted this as Iran's attempts to access Zimbabwe's uranium and diamonds.

In April, Chinese Vice Prime Minister Hui Liangyu visited Zimbabwe. He held talks with Tsvangirai, who stated that Zimbabwe would keep its "all-weather" friendly relationship with China whatever happened in the future. In December, Mugabe visited *China* and met with Hui Liangyu. The two countries reaffirmed their friendship and pledged continued cooperation. On 27 October, in an interview in 'The Herald', the Chinese ambassador to Zimbabwe asserted that the two countries enjoyed a profound traditional friendship and that China would stand by Zimbabwe.

South Korea, which had an embassy in Harare and had signed a bilateral investment treaty with Zimbabwe, continued to make its presence felt. On 20 February, at an event to hand over shoes, balls and food to a ZANU-PF representative, its diplomatic representative said the donation would go a long way in strengthening relations between the two countries.

Socioeconomic Developments

There were indications that the huge improvement in *economic indicators* witnessed since the launch of the GNU was beginning to moderate. Reserve Bank of Zimbabwe (RBZ) figures showed that the consumer price index marginally increased to 102.9%, with the year-on-year price increase at 2.90%. According to Economist Intelligence Unit (EIU) estimates, real GDP growth was 2.1%. The national budget unveiled in November revised the growth forecasts to 4.4%, down from 5.6% in July. The EIU put the nominal GDP at $ 2.3 bn, up from $ 2.0 bn in 2011. Manufacturing grew by only 2.1%. The low growth was explained by a lack of investment and excessive imports.

The current account balance, excluding transfers, was –$ 0.6 bn compared with $ 58.6 m in 2011, while total international reserves dropped from $ 461 m to $ 422 m. In the budget statement, the finance minister put the external debt at more than $ 10 bn. The country continued to be in default, with arrears then estimated at $ 6.1 bn. The expected windfall from *diamonds* did not materialise, as revenue from the minerals did not live up to expectations. On 6 November, the Zimbabwe Mining Development Corporation announced that the diamond industry was expected to contribute only a quarter of the $ 600 m that Treasury had projected would come from the sector in 2012.

Zimbabwe performed poorly in a number of *World Bank league tables*. The country was ranked 171st out of 183 economies in 'Doing Business 2012', Zimbabwe's overall score having fallen by three points, reflecting lower scores for five indicators. The most drastic drop occurred in the Getting Credit indicator, where it fell ten places. Zimbabwe's economic freedom score was 26.3, making its economy the 178th freest in the 2012 Index. Its score had increased by 4.2 points from 2011, reflecting gains in half of the ten economic freedoms. Zimbabwe was ranked last out of 46 countries in the Sub-Saharan Africa region and was the second least free country ranked in the 2012 Index.

According to a Reliefweb appeal published on 23 November, the *humanitarian situation* continued to improve and was largely stable. However, humanitarian challenges remained. Among them were food insecurity and sporadic outbreaks of waterborne diseases. Not surprisingly, a wide range of highly vulnerable groups, such as the chronically ill, returned migrants, asylum seekers and people in displacement-like situations, continued to require humanitarian aid.

Food security remained a concern. According to WFP, cereal production for the 2011–2012 season was 1,076,772 metric tonnes – a third lower than in the previous season. At the beginning of the year, crop-planting figures suggested that output of maize, cotton and soya would decline. The Zimbabwe Vulnerability Assessment Committee (ZimVAC) estimated that 1.6 m 'food-insecure' people would be unable to meet their basic food requirements in the 2012/13 consumption year until the time of the following harvest in April 2013. WFP identified the threats to food security as including political and economic instability, recurrent droughts, poverty, poor agricultural practices, HIV/AIDS and high unemployment. The agency reported that, together with its partners, it was responding to the crisis by providing Targeted Seasonal Assistance to meet the food needs of highly vulnerable groups during the lean season.

Throughout the year, there were reports of *outbreaks of typhoid* in the cities. On 24 January, the authorities revealed that more than 660 people had been treated for typhoid in Harare. They claimed that the outbreak of the bacterial disease appeared to be waning. In July, at least 111 cases of typhoid were reported in Harare and Chitungwiza. City of Harare officials said the outbreak was due to water shortages in the city and in the satellite towns of Chitungwiza, Norton, Ruwa and Epworth. In December, the Combined Harare Residents Association warned that water from unprotected wells in the suburbs of Dzivaresekwa, Mufakose, Budiriro, Glen View and Highfields contained salmonella-typhea, a bacterium that caused typhoid.

Progress was reported in the country's response to *HIV/AIDS*. According to the 2010–11 Zimbabwe Demographic and Health Survey (ZDHS), 15% of Zimbabweans were HIV-positive. This was a slight decrease from 18% in the 2005–6 ZDHS survey. HIV prevalence continued to be higher among women than men: 18% of women were HIV-positive compared with 12% of men. A third of women in their thirties and a third of men in their forties were HIV-positive. Over half of widowed women and men were HIV-positive. The number of people living with HIV was between 1.2 m and 1.3 m. HIV prevalence was highest in Matabeleland South, where 21% of adults (aged 15–49) were reported to be HIV-positive. Harare registered the lowest rate at 13%. In addition, the report showed that mosquito net ownership and use had increased three-fold; fertility had increased to 4.1 from 3.8 in 2005–6; 57% of married women were using a modern method of contraception; two-thirds of births occurred in health facilities; and two-thirds of births were assisted by a skilled provider.

Despite some marked improvements, the *education and health* delivery systems continued to experience problems of staffing, equipment and funding. Health and educational personnel continued to constitute a substantial part of the brain drain. Industrial action and threats of industrial action arising out of salary disputes were a constant feature, further compromising these sectors. On 6 January, the government suspended the 'bonding' of nurses with immediate effect until it had the capacity to employ them. In August, the government indicated that it had formalised plans to export some 2,000 nurses to other countries. The country had been unable to employ all the nurses it trained, but had continued to bond them, resulting in their being jobless but at the same time unable to be seek employment elsewhere. According to official sources, many countries including Swaziland, Lesotho, Trinidad and Tobago had indicated that they needed hundreds of nurses to work in their countries under a government-to-government agreement.

The *indigenisation* drive continued to be a controversial and polarising issue. A number of mining companies, among them the mining giant Zimplats, had their indigenisation plans accepted by the Ministry of Youth Development, Indigenisation and Empowerment. Others had theirs rejected or modified. Zimplats was the first mining company to implement the indigenisation process by launching a shared ownership scheme for the Mhondoro-Ngezi, Chegutu and Zvimba communities. In February, Youth Development, Indigenisation and Empowerment Minister Saviour Kasukuwere advised the mining company Mimosa that a portion of its indigenisation proposals had been rejected. The government also ordered Impala Platinum to transfer 29.5% of its shares to the National Indigenisation and Economic Empowerment Fund in order to comply with local empowerment laws. Throughout the year, Kasukuwere issued a stream of threats to foreign-owned banks. The MDC-T continued to publicly disagree with the programme. In what was interpreted as a symptom of the infighting within ZANU-PF, RBZ governor Gideon Gono publicly differed with Kasukuwere on the indigenisation of banks.

There was no let-up in the dismal performance of *parastatals*. The state carrier, Air Zimbabwe, which was virtually grounded for the whole year due to crippling debts, obtained two new aircraft despite its perilous financial position. In December, Air Zimbabwe confirmed that it had received two A320 Airbus planes, which would operate at the beginning of 2013 in the company's attempt to return to its regional and international routes. The steel maker Ziscosteel remained in a poor state. In October, it was reported that the Indian company Essar, which had signed a $ 750 m deal to take over the troubled steel maker, was yet to commence operations due to bickering over the control of minerals to be used as feedstock for the project and demands that the project should be in line with the country's indigenisation policy. In October, reports indicated that the National Railways of Zimbabwe had failed to pay its 7,000 employees for the previous five months. The company needed $ 400 m to upgrade its infrastructure, as it tried to boost its cargo carriage.

On 15 November, Finance Minister Tendai Biti presented the 2013 *national budget*, which he described as the fifth and last budget of the GNU. Biti proposed a $ 3.8 bn budget. Its most notable feature was that civil servants' salaries accounted for 73% of the budget. Biti projected a growth rate of 4.4% for 2013. Agricultural growth was revised down from 5.5% to 4.6%. He said the budget was inspired by the need for economic growth and job creation. Biti lamented the fact that imports remained very high for a small economy like Zimbabwe's. He said growth momentum would be underpinned by expansion in the finance, mining, tourism, agriculture, manufacturing and transport sectors.

At midnight on 17 August, the official *national census* kicked off. It was marred by controversy. Soldiers threatened to take over the task by force. The census had been in danger of being cancelled the previous week after thousands of soldiers around the country had stormed centres where enumerators (mostly teachers) had gathered for the final session of their three-month training. They were apparently motivated by the allowances that came with the job. The results released in December showed that the population had increased by an annual inter-censal growth rate of 1.1% since the 2002 census. The population of Zimbabwe on August 18 was 12,973,808. The results were queried by, among others, the Progressive Teacher's Union of Zimbabwe (PTUZ) and Bulawayo City Council, who claimed that the results underestimated population and growth. According to the census figures Bulawayo had a population of 655,675. The city's mayor argued that the actual population was 1.5 m. The PTUZ supported Bulawayo's assertions, claiming that the figures had been manipulated by the Central Intelligence Organisation, the military and ZANU-PF in an effort to limit voter registration in areas where ZANU-PF would have little support in the forthcoming election. There was an indication that Zimbabwe's exodus had marginally slowed down. The estimated net migration rate was 23.8 migrants per 1,000 of the population. There was, however, an increasing flow of Zimbabweans into South Africa and Botswana in search of better economic opportunities.

Zimbabwe in 2013

The year saw the end of the Government of National Unity (GNU). A new constitution came into existence. The first half of the year was dominated by a controversial election, which was resoundingly won by the Zimbabwe African National Union-Patriotic Front (ZANU-PF). The second half saw Zimbabwe drifting back into economic problems. There were no significant shifts in international relations or socio-economic developments.

Domestic Politics

After months of wrangling and brinkmanship, on 17 January ZANU-PF and the two factions of the Movement for Democratic Change (MDC) finally agreed on a *draft constitution*, paving the way for the much-awaited referendum. President Robert Mugabe called this "the end of a marathon exercise", while MDC-T leader Morgan Tsvangirai labelled it "a defining moment for the country". The government had *funding problems* for both the election and the referendum. On 30 January, it was reported that principals in the GNU had tasked Justice and Legal Affairs Minister Patrick Chinamasa and Finance Minister Tendai Biti with sourcing money for the referendum and general elections from donors. About $ 85 m was needed for the referendum, while elections required $ 107 m. The Zimbabwe Electoral Commission (ZEC) had budgeted $ 220 m for the two events. The reduction in the budget was a result of the abandonment of the delimitation exercise. On 11 March, Tendai Biti announced that Zimbabwe had issued a bond to raise funds for the referendum.

The *referendum* on the new constitution was held on 19 March, with all three GNU parties uncharacteristically on the same side, urging a 'yes' vote. The National Constitutional Assembly, which had

 | DOI:10.1163/9789004404335_007

unsuccessfully sought to delay the referendum, campaigned against the constitution, claiming it was not democratic and people-driven. There were concerns about the financing of the referendum. When the results were declared, the ZEC announced that the new constitution had been approved by an overwhelming majority of 3 m votes. Nearly 95% of those who participated had voted 'yes'. One of the key provisions of the new constitution was the limiting future presidents to two five-year terms. It also increased the number of legislators from 210 to 270, with 60 seats reserved for women.

On 22 May, Mugabe signed the *new constitution* into law, replacing the 1979 Lancaster House Constitution. This unleashed a wave of speculation and debate on the *election date*, which ZANU-PF wanted to be early. The new constitution required that a 30-day mandatory voter registration period be scheduled from the day the new constitution was published, while 56 days would be needed from the day the election date was decreed to the polling date. This meant ZANU-PF's target of holding the election when the GNU's term expired on 29 June would not be possible. This gave rise to debates, accusations and counteraccusations, with ZANU-PF insisting the 29 June date was feasible and some critics and experts maintaining the latest the election could be held was 31 October. ZANU-PF's insistence on an early date fuelled speculation, ranging from charges that ZANU-PF had a strategy to take advantage of the MDCs' lack of preparedness to suspicions that there were plots to rig the poll. ZANU-PF's desire for an early election date might have been driven by reports that the MDC-T was losing support. In a Freedom House-commissioned poll released in February, the Mass Public Opinion Institute reported that ZANU-PF support stood at 31%, up from 17% in 2010, with support for the MDC dropping from 38% in 2010 to 20%. On 4 May, the MDC-T rubbished the opinion poll, claiming the party would pick up 75% of the vote.

On 31 May, a landmark *Constitutional Court ruling* delivered by Chief Justice Godfrey Chidyausiku compelled President Mugabe to announce an election date by July 31. The person behind the court application was Jealousy Mawarire, whom the MDC-T claimed was a ZANU-PF stooge. In compliance with the court ruling, in a Government Gazette on 12 June, Mugabe unilaterally declared 31 July as the date for the harmonised national election, which immediately set him at loggerheads with Prime Minister Morgan Tsvangirai. On 13 June, an Extraordinary Government Gazette stated that the nomination court would sit on 28 June. Predictably, these unilaterally fixed dates became a source of tension and controversy among the GNU partners. Mugabe claimed he had been forced to set the dates by a court ruling and joined Tsvangirai in approaching the courts to have the elections postponed. There was widespread scepticism of Mugabe's sincerity, with claims that he was half-hearted in what was seen as his tokenistic pursuit of the case. This was interpreted as a strategy to outwit the MDCs, which appeared to be confirmed when, during the hearing of the case, the justice minister's attorney announced that the minister was abandoning his application to have the election date extended to 14 August. Tsvangirai's lawyer told the court the elections should be conducted under new electoral laws that would have to be passed through parliament in line with provisions of the new constitution. On 4 July, the Constitutional Court rejected the appeal to delay the elections. The ruling declared that the elections would proceed on 31 July in line with Mugabe's proclamation. As expected, both MDC factions were unhappy with the ruling, while the state media and ZANU-PF apologists welcomed it and flaunted it as confirmation that the rule of law prevailed in Zimbabwe.

In the run-up to the election, there was speculation about whether the two MDCs would be entering into an *anti-Mugabe election coalition*. While Tsvangirai appeared eager to forge a united front, Welshman Ncube, leader of the MDC-N, was reported to have dismissed coalition talks. On 21 April, Ncube defended his party's position, saying that, if they did not make a stand, Zimbabwe would be replacing one dictator with another. In the end, Ncube entered into a pact with Dumiso Dabengwa's Zimbabwe African People's

Union (ZAPU), while Tsvangirai forged an alliance with former finance minister Simba Makoni's Mavambo/Kusile/Dawn and ZANU Ndonga. On 23 July, Ncube said he was yet to be approached by Tsvangirai's MDC about an anti-Mugabe coalition. He dismissed Tsvangirai's suggestion that Ncube did not want an alliance, calling it "the politics of deception". Commentators attributed the failure to forge an alliance to the political egos of the key players.

The *election campaign* was predictably acrimonious, with the usual accusations of violence and rigging being made by the MDC-T and ZANU-PF responding with characteristic denials and counteraccusations. The largely peaceful pre-election period was occasionally marred by reports of politically motivated violence in some rural areas. According to monitors, there was less violence than 2008, but there were reports of intimidation by pro-ZANU-PF supporters, militia and security personnel in the countryside. *Nikuv International Projects* (NIP), a secretive Israel-based company, featured prominently in the MDC-T's campaigns and in general public speculation, with allegations that it might be the key player in ZANU-PF's strategy to rig the elections. NIP, which specialises in population registration and election systems, had previously been accused of manipulating elections in the region. It was alleged to be involved in managing the electoral roll in cahoots with the Central Intelligence Organisation with a view to rigging the election in ZANU-PF's favour. The ZEC was also caught up in the speculation and was repeatedly warned by Tsvangirai against being involved in attempts to rig the poll. Tsvangirai confidently declared that the scale of the MDC-T's victory would make any rigging irrelevant.

The election was peaceful. When the election results were announced, ZANU-PF claimed massive victories in both the presidential and parliamentary elections. In the *presidential poll*, Mugabe won 60.6% of the vote, with Tsvangirai coming a distant second with 33.7%; Ncube was third with 2.7%. There were two other candidates: Dumiso Dabengwa of ZAPU got 0.7% and little known Kisinoti Mukwazhe got 0.3%. About 2% of the ballots were spoilt.

In the *parliamentary vote*, ZANU-PF took 160 seats and the MDC-T 49, while an independent candidate won the remaining seat. With the proportional representation seats reserved for women, the election resulted in the following distribution of seats in the National Assembly: ZANU-PF 197, MDC-T 70, MDC-N 2, Independent 1. In the Senate, ZANU-PF, MDC-T and MDC-N took 37, 21 and 2 seats, respectively.

This was yet another *controversial election*. The MDCs unsurprisingly rejected the results, claiming the election had been massively rigged. Describing the election as "a huge farce", Tsvangirai said the nation was in mourning over the results. He claimed that over a million voters had been turned away from the polling stations and promised to fight the results legally and diplomatically. While ZANU-PF, its apologists and the state media quickly pronounced the election both free and fair, there were unclear signals from the cherry-picked observers. Many endorsed the freeness of the poll, but there was no agreement on its fairness. The AU observer mission on 2 August cryptically pronounced the election free and fair "from the campaigning point of view", and declared the elections "free, honest and credible". Notably, the mission stated that there were irregularities, but added that they were not of such a scale as to affect the election outcome. SADC observers agreed that the elections were free but did not declare them fair. On 1 August, the Zimbabwe Election Support Network (ZESN) – by far the largest group of domestic monitors with some 7,000 people on the ground across the country – stated that the elections were "seriously compromised". Echoing Tsvangirai's assertions, the group claimed that some 1 m voters had been unable to cast their ballots. According to ZESN, potential voters were much more likely to have been turned away from polling stations in MDC-T urban strongholds than in ZANU-PF's rural strongholds. The group further alleged significant pre-election irregularities, claiming that 99.7% of rural voters were registered on the electoral roll in June compared with only 67.9% of urban voters. On 8 August, the ZEC admitted mistakes, saying that 305,000 voters had been turned away and 207,000 other voters had received help when they marked their ballots. But the commission stuck to its original statement that the election was free and fair.

In a *legal challenge*, on 9 August Tsvangirai asked the Constitutional Court to nullify the controversial elections, arguing that he could have won if all his supporters had been allowed to vote. On 13 August, the High Court heard petitions by Tsvangirai for the ZEC to release voting data and related material to help back his main legal challenge to the elections. On 16 August, however, Tsvangirai announced that he had withdrawn his court case challenging Mugabe's re-election. In an affidavit filed at the Constitutional Court, Tsvangirai gave his reason for this as the ZEC's refusal to release the election material he wanted to use in the court case. However, the Constitutional Court pressed ahead with the case, declaring that a petition challenging a presidential election "cannot be terminated by a withdrawal". On 20 August, Chief Justice Godfrey Chidyausiku handed down the unanimous decision of the Constitutional Court dismissing Tsvangirai's election petition. On the same day, it was announced by High Court judge Chinembiri Bhunu that Tsvangirai might face contempt of court charges for "disparaging remarks" he had made about the judiciary. The electoral court ordered the attorney general to investigate charges of contempt of court against Tsvangirai's lawyers for submitting – as part of its petition claims – that court judges were under the influence of ZANU-PF. Mugabe was sworn in as president on 22 August. By the end of the year, the MDC-T had not conceded defeat, and still regarded Mugabe's presidency as illegitimate.

On 10 September, Mugabe appointed a slightly trimmed *cabinet* of 26 members, down from 33 in the GNU. Largely recycled, it was a combination of hardliners and moderates. Significantly, the indigenisation and mining portfolios previously held by hardliners went to moderates, with Francis Nhema taking over the indigenisation portfolio and Walter Chidhakwa being appointed mining minister. In what was widely interpreted as a demotion, Saviour Kasukuwere, the militant former indigenisation minister, was moved to environment and tourism, and Obert Mpofu was moved to transport and infrastructure development. The finance ministry went to former justice minister Patrick Chinamasa. Emerson Mnangagwa, seen as a possible successor to Mugabe, was transferred from defence to justice. Another possible successor, Joice Mujuru, retained the vice presidency. Jonathan Moyo returned to the Ministry of Information.

The remaining year was dominated by the controversy surrounding the election and a return to intra-party politics. In November, it was reported that *factional fighting* had resurfaced in ZANU-PF. The public mudslinging was ignited by contentious provincial elections, seen as crucial in the succession saga. Elections for provincial chairmen in Manicaland, Midlands and Mashonaland Central were marred by allegations of vote rigging. As expected, the conflicts were between the Mujuru and Mnangagwa factions. There were public disagreements over the Mashonaland provincial elections between presidential spokesperson George Charamba and ZANU-PF secretary for administration Didymus Mutasa, a known Mujuru loyalist. Jonathan Moyo waded into the fight, defending Charamba. Tension had been bubbling below the surface for a long time as the feuding factions continued positioning themselves to take over from Mugabe.

ZANU-PF held its *14th National People's Conference* in Chinhoyi on 12–14 December under the theme 'ZIMASSET: Growing the Economy for Empowerment and Employment'. Some 7,000 delegates attended. Factional fighting reportedly intensified. Mugabe denounced divisions in the ruling party as factions positioned themselves in the on-going battle for the succession. Mugabe said that ZANU-PF could not build a united party "when we divide people into camps of those who belong to so-and-so and those who belong to so-and-so". The conference resolutions were the usual patriotic statements and calls for improvements in areas such as agriculture, social services, poverty eradication, infrastructure and utilities. Unsurprisingly, the 'illegal sanctions' imposed by 'Western imperialist countries' featured prominently. Interestingly, the party acknowledged factionalism but blamed it on the Western forces that were seeking illegal regime change. The party resolved to guard against these "uncanny machinations by the Western imperialists through factionalism and other divisive stratagems as new regime change tools".

Foreign Affairs

Zimbabwe's relations with the majority of African and Asian countries and organisations continued to be friendly. Relations with Western countries, which had appeared to be thawing despite the persistent 'illegal' sanctions mantra, dramatically worsened as Western countries publicly condemned the controversial elections. *SADC* continued its active involvement in Zimbabwe. A SADC summit on Zimbabwe's upcoming elections and funding, scheduled for Maputo (Mozambique) on 9 June, was inexplicably cancelled. There were reports that Mugabe had indicated he could not go to Maputo as he had more pressing election-related constitutional matters to attend to. Mugabe's office was at pains to explain that the president was not contemptuous of SADC, nor was he resisting the regional bloc's facilitation. In the run-up to the elections, Mugabe had become hostile to the regional bloc and, in an apparent threat to pull Zimbabwe out of SADC, he said on 6 July that Zimbabwe was in SADC voluntarily and could walk out of the organisation if it decided "to do stupid things". He was unhappy with SADC's facilitation role.

In their final report, released on 2 September, the SADC observer mission concluded that the elections had been "free, peaceful and generally credible", but crucially admitted that some irregularities cast doubt on their fairness. Although this was not the ringing endorsement that ZANU-PF needed, state media and ZANU-PF apologists used the statement to their advantage. In contrast to the SADC observer mission's ambivalence, the *SADC Council of NGOs* concluded that the scope and extent of the impact of the observed anomalies on the outcome of elections constituted "serious electoral deficits". This mission concluded that the credibility, legitimacy and free and fair conduct of the elections, and their reliability as the true expression of the will of the people of Zimbabwe had been highly compromised. In stark opposition to this, the SADC *Parliamentary Forum* Election Observation Mission to the elections concluded that the elections were "on the whole, a credible reflection of the will of the people of Zimbabwe" and declared the elections to have been free and fair. At the SADC *Summit* in Lilongwe (Malawi) on 18 August, the Heads of States and Governments endorsed Mugabe's electoral victory and called for the West to lift all sanctions imposed on Zimbabwe, with Malawi's President Banda saying Zimbabweans had suffered enough.

Zimbabwe's *relations with South Africa* were mixed. At times there was evidence of testy relations between Mugabe and President Zuma. There was speculation that ZANU-PF would have liked Zuma to be defeated at the ANC's 53rd Annual Conference in Mangaung in December 2012 and that ZANU-PF was working with expelled former ANC youth leader Julius Malema to undermine Zuma. In what was interpreted as a thinly veiled attack on Zuma, Mugabe said on 20 July that African countries should not spread lies about Zimbabwe. This came after Zuma had criticised Zimbabwe's preparations for the elections, saying the process was "not looking good". Mugabe expressed his reservations on Zuma's facilitation role, and publicly attacked Zuma's special adviser, Lindiwe Zulu, urging Zuma to call her to order. Mugabe had earlier insulted Zulu, calling her a "streetwalker" and "stupid idiotic woman". This came after she had indicated that SADC was looking for a one-month delay in the elections. On 4 August, Zuma congratulated Mugabe on his re-election, urging all political parties to accept the outcome of the polls. Despite the occasional public spats, South Africa continued to help Zimbabwe. On 25 January, a South African court temporarily halted a delivery of helicopters to the Zimbabwean military after a challenge by human rights group AfriForum. The group had made the urgent request following reports of a donation of South Africa's retired Alouette fleet. AfriForum was against giving the equipment to a force that it argued was not neutral. The South African defence ministry had indicated that the aircraft would be used only for spare parts. On 15 April, Finance Minister Tendai Biti announced that South Africa had approved $ 100 m in budgetary support to Zimbabwe. The money would help fund the poll.

After what had appeared to be a softening of its critical stance, *Botswana* again broke ranks with the rest of SADC on Zimbabwe by publicly rejecting the results of the elections. On 5 August, it called for an independent audit of the disputed poll, saying the elections could not be considered acceptably free and fair. Even after the SADC leaders' endorsement of the poll, Botswana maintained that its position had not changed. In contrast, Zimbabwe's relations with *Malawi* remained cordial. Despite having been close to Malawian President Joyce Banda's late adversary, Mugabe invited Banda to open the Zimbabwe International Trade Fair on 26 May. President Michael Sata of *Zambia* remained a close ally of Mugabe and promised in May to send 150,000 tonnes of maize to help drought-stricken Zimbabwe. Mugabe saluted Sata, describing him as a "grand man".

Relations with the EU appeared to have improved marginally at the beginning of the year, but deteriorated after the elections. On 5 March, state media announced that Mugabe had declared that Zimbabwe would not invite Western observers for the constitutional referendum and general election. The official reason given for this was the Western 'illegal' sanctions. As expected, the decision inevitably triggered a dispute in the GNU. On 25 March, the EU suspended sanctions against 81 officials and eight companies in Zimbabwe. According to the EU statement, this decision was based on the conclusion of a "peaceful, successful and credible" referendum. The bloc still maintained its sanctions against Mugabe, nine senior ZANU-PF people and two companies. Following the announcement of the election results, the EU said it was concerned about alleged irregularities and reports of incomplete participation, as well as the identified weaknesses in the electoral process and a lack of transparency. On 22 August, the EU announced it would review relations with Zimbabwe given its "serious concerns" about the conduct of the elections.

Zimbabwe's relations with Western countries did not improve, not helped by their reaction to the conduct and results of the disputed elections, which the West had not been allowed to monitor. In a statement on 3 August, the *USA* said that the balance of evidence indicated that the announcement of the results was the "culmination of a deeply flawed process", citing irregularities relating to the electoral roll, unequal access to state media, a partisan security sector, and failure to implement the political reforms mandated by the new constitution, the Global Policy Agreement, and SADC. Relations with the *UK* remained similarly tense. This was not helped when, on 3 August, the Foreign and Commonwealth Office expressed concerns about the conduct of the elections, indicating that they had not been free, fair and credible. On 4 August, *Australia* also raised doubts about the credibility of the election results, saying that the remaining sanctions on Zimbabwe would continue. On 3 August, *Canada* expressed serious concerns about the reported irregularities and lack of transparency in the democratic process, stating these called into question whether the results could credibly represent the will of the people. On 26 September, in his speech to the 68th UN General Assembly in New York, Mugabe berated the USA and the UK for imposing "illegal and filthy sanctions" on Zimbabwe. The US delegation walked out.

Good relations with traditional allies in the east continued. Among those invited to monitor the elections were Iran and *China*, who promptly endorsed the results as soon as they were announced. In May, the Ministry of Energy and Power Development announced that a major Chinese bank had agreed to finance construction of the Hwange thermal power station. However, it remained unclear which Chinese bank would provide the funding and what portion of the production costs would be covered. On 11 November, Finance Minister Chinamasa announced that China would lend Zimbabwe $ 320 m to pay for the expansion of the Kariba hydropower station. However, China did not seem too enthusiastic: in November, Chinamasa went to China looking for budgetary support but came back empty-handed. Later in the month, it was revealed that Zimbabwe was seeking a $ 10 bn bailout from China to kick-start the economy, and in the same month it was reported that officials from the government and the Reserve Bank of Zimbabwe (RBZ) were in China seeking to negotiate a $ 4 bn loan. By the end of the year, the loan and bailout had not materialised. On 10 August, the then deputy mining minister, Gift Chimanikire revealed that a deal had been struck between *Iran* and the Zimbabwe government that would see Zimbabwe exporting uranium to Iran. Zimbabwe dismissed the report, denying that there was ever such a deal. In July, Education and Sports Minister David Coltart announced he was vising *South Korea* for bilateral talks to get Korean maths and science teachers to teach in Zimbabwean schools. It was not clear what trajectory relations would take in post-GNU Zimbabwe.

Relations with multilateral financial institutions were mixed. In September, the *AfDB* said the IMF-supervised economic reform was indicative of the significant improvement in Zimbabwe's cooperation on economic policies and its commitment to address its arrear problems. Earlier in July, the bank had launched a $ 24 m capacity-building project for public finance and economic management as Zimbabwe stepped up efforts to tackle its $ 10.7 bn external debt. As at 31 December, overdue payments to the *IMF* amounted to $ 81.7 m of which $ 16.5 m were charges and interest. In July, the IMF concluded that Zimbabwe remained in debt distress, with total external debt estimated at 88% of GDP, of which 50% of GDP was in arrears. According to the IMF, the external arrears continued to stifle economic growth by limiting the country's access to new financing. The *World Bank*'s lending programme in Zimbabwe remained inactive due to arrears, with the bank's role limited to technical assistance and analytical work.

Socioeconomic Developments

The economy seemed to get into trouble after the election. However, on average there was no huge decline in stability and no sharp decline in *economic indicators*. RBZ figures showed that the all prices consumer price index fell marginally to 100.3%, down from 102.9% in 2012. The year-on-year price increase was 0.3%. According to Economist Intelligence Unit (EIU) estimates, the real GDP growth was 2.2%. The national budget unveiled in December revised growth forecasts down to 3.4% from an earlier 5.5% projection. The national budget was presented later than usual because the government was looking for budgetary support. The EIU put the nominal GDP at $ 2.5 bn, up from $ 2.3 bn in 2012. Manufacturing declined by 5.3%. The low growth was attributed to lack of investment and excessive imports. The current account balance was –$ 0.6 bn up from –$ 416 m in 2012, while total international reserves dropped from $ 576 m in 2012 to $ 437 m. In the budget statement, the finance minister put the external debt at more than $ 10 bn. The external debt stock dropped marginally from $ 7,388 m to $ 7,088 m. The stock of accumulated arrears accounted for $ 4.72 bn, making up 78% of total debt stock. On 30 January, Finance Minister Tendai Biti announced that the country had only $ 217 left in its public account the previous week, after paying civil servants. He explained that he was making this revelation to show that the country had no money to finance the election. On 11 March, Biti announced that Zimbabwe had raised $ 40 m from a special bond floated to the local unit of Old Mutual and the state pension fund to help finance the constitutional referendum. He said the one-year bond would attract an interest rate of 7%.

On 22 October, the cabinet adopted the Zimbabwe Agenda for Sustainable Socio-Economic Transformation (*ZimAsset*), a five-year development programme extracted from ZANU-PF's election manifesto, aimed at transforming the country's economic fortunes and increasing growth from 6.1% in 2014 to 9.9% by 2018. An important feature of the programme was the proposal to leverage the country's natural resources to source external capital. The economic road map would run from October 2013 to December 2018.

Zimbabwe performed poorly in a number of *international league tables*. It was ranked 173rd out of 185 economies in the annual Doing Business survey and was ranked 172nd in the UNDP's Human Development Report with an HDI of 0.397, putting the country in the low human development category. The country also fared badly on some *individual indicators*. The poverty headcount ratio was 72%; average life expectancy remained fairly low at 52.7 years; and gross national income per capita in PPP terms was $ 424. However, at 90.7%, Zimbabwe's literacy rate remained the highest in Africa and among the highest in the global South.

No major economic changes with implications for the humanitarian situation occurred during the first half of the year. In terms of *food security*, prolonged dry spells and erratic rainfall patterns affected agricultural production. According to the results of the Zimbabwe Vulnerability Committee Assessment (ZimVAC) appraisal, 25% of rural households were projected to be food insecure at the peak of the agricultural season. This was a 32% increase in food insecure people compared to the previous season and represented 2.2 m people at peak hunger season not being able to meet their annual food requirements. On 11 June, UN agencies reported that Zimbabwe would require at least $ 131 m in aid, the bulk for food assistance after a failed farming season left nearly 1.7 m people facing hunger.

Public health issues during the year included typhoid, diarrheal disease and suspected cholera outbreaks, as well as floods in 12 rural districts and six urban localities in six provinces. Typhoid cases carried over from 2012, together with high levels of diarrhoea within the first half of the year, pointing to inadequacies in the provision of water, sanitation and hygiene promotion services. According to the Ministry of Health and Child Welfare weekly report for the week ending 8 December, there were 85 cases of typhoid in the country. Malaria outbreaks left 370 people dead, with 428,320 others treated for the disease. The government embarked on a national programme that saw all children under the age of 15 receiving praziquantel and albendazole for treatment of intestinal worms and bilharzia. Progress was reported in the country's response to *HIV/AIDS*. According to the National AIDS Council, 15% of Zimbabweans were HIV-positive. The estimated adult HIV incidence (15–49 years) was 0.831. The estimated number of people living with HIV was 1,242,768, with 58,472 new infections. The estimated number of AIDS orphans was 941,024. The anti-retroviral treatment (ART) coverage was 86.1%.

Despite some improvements, the *education sector* continued to experience problems with staffing, equipment and funding, although some funding was provided by the Education Transition Fund, a mechanism to allow donors control over their funds. In 2013, $ 25 m was earmarked for the fund, up from $ 12 m in 2012. There are some 106,000 teachers in the country and about 30,000 more were required. Threats of strikes haunted the sector throughout the year. As early as January, the Zimbabwe Teachers' Association, the largest union of teachers, announced it had lined up annual general meetings at provincial level across the country to discuss, among other things, deteriorating conditions of service for members. The more combative Progressive Teacher's Union regularly threatened to take strike action. The state-controlled media was supportive of the unions' tough stance and threats, interpreting these as a condemnation of the MDCs, whose ministers were responsible for education (MDC-N) and finance (MDC-T) in the GNU.

In September, it was reported that the Bankers' Association of Zimbabwe had set aside $ 620 m to *finance agriculture*. Individual farmers and suppliers were free to access the funds. Earlier, CBZ Bank had secured $ 100 m from the African Export and Import Bank to support agriculture. On 2 October, Chinamasa announced $ 161 m support for agriculture. The facility would be for the government's input support programme targeting 1.6 m communal, old resettled, small-scale and A1 farmers. This brought the total support package for agriculture to nearly $ 1 bn.

The *indigenisation drive* continued to be a controversial and polarising issue, even within ZANU-PF. Before the election, there was public disagreement between the minister of youth development, indigenisation and empowerment and the RBZ governor over the indenisation of banks, with the former seemingly protecting the sector. On 11 January, Impala Platinum Holdings (Implats) subsidiary Zimplats agreed to sell a 51% stake in its platinum operations to indigenous entities in Zimbabwe for $ 971 m, bringing the company in line with the country's indigenisation plan.

On 19 December, Finance Minister Chinamasa presented the 2014 national *budget* amounting to $ 4.2 bn. Recurrent expenditure accounted for 73%. Notably, cumulative expenditure to November had amounted to $ 3.5 bn against a target of $ 3.4 bn, resulting in expenditure overrun of $ 130 m. Total revenue collections up to November amounted to $ 3.36 bn, against a target of $ 3.4 bn, resulting in a negative variance of $ 35 m. In an apparent response to widespread speculation about the return of the Zimbabwe dollar, Chinamasa reiterated that the economy would continue using the multiple currency regime.

Zimbabwe's controversial *Marange diamonds* were in the news for most of the year. In June, the mines and energy portfolio committee raised the alarm about the lack of accountability for the sale and smuggling of diamonds from Marange. This was costing the treasury hundreds of millions of dollars in lost revenue. On 17 September, in a move spearheaded by Belgium, the EU agreed to lift sanctions on the state-owned diamond-mining firm the Zimbabwe Mining Development Corporation (ZMDC). Belgium said lifting EU sanctions on ZMDC would increase Zimbabwe's tax revenues by $ 400 m a year. In December, it was reported that Zimbabwe was to auction 300,000 carats of diamonds in the EU. On 13 December, mining company DTZ-OZ GEO announced it had found conglomerate deposits capable of producing 2.5 m carats of top quality diamonds in the Chimanimani area.

Zimbabwe in 2014

During the year, factional fights in both major parties were played out in the open. While the succession war in the Zimbabwe African National Union-Patriotic Front (ZANU-PF) seemed to have produced a victor – at least for the time being – the conflicts in the fractured and weakened opposition Movement for Democratic Change-Tsvangirai (MDC-T) raised more questions than answers. There was no substantive shift on the foreign affairs scene, the only movement being the lifting of targeted sanctions on some individuals and companies. The economy did not perform well, with critics and commentators indicating that the country was rapidly sliding back to the harrowing meltdown of 2008. 'Illegal' Western sanctions continued to be government's favourite scapegoat for the economic woes.

Domestic Politics

Relations between the major political parties remained strained as acrimonious exchanges, name-calling, accusations and counteraccusations persisted. The MDC-T continued to insist that the 2013 elections were rigged, with Morgan Tsvangirai characteristically refusing to recognise Robert Mugabe as the legitimate president. The bad blood came to the fore early in the year when the parties clashed over the passing of the Electoral Amendment Bill. The Bill was gazetted on 3 January. It aimed at aligning the Electoral Act with the new constitution. The Bill was fast tracked through parliament and was passed by the ZANU-PF-dominated house on 4 January. The MDC-T raised concerns that the amendments did not go far enough to guarantee free and fair elections and this view was echoed by other critics of the regime. They accused ZANU-PF of seeking to re-introduce postal voting, bar Zimbabweans in the diaspora from

 | DOI:10.1163/9789004404335_008

voting, legalise the use of voter registration slips and deny automatic access to the voters' roll. These issues had already been at the heart of the acrimony in the poisoned electoral landscape in 2013.

The MDC-T was rocked by internal disagreements and a *struggle for supremacy*, which apparently started when deputy treasurer general and former energy minister Elton Mangoma, in a letter to Tsvangirai, called for leadership renewal. Mangoma urged Tsvangirai to "consider leaving the office of the president of the movement", under a plan to restore hope and confidence in the party. The letter was reproduced in the state mouthpiece, 'The Herald', on 27 January and tore the opposition party apart. While ZANU-PF and the state-controlled media hailed Mangoma's letter, its reception in the MDC-T was decidedly hostile. Mangoma claimed he was a victim of violence within the party. On 31 January, the MDC-T National Executive formally censured Mangoma and passed a resolution branding him "MDC in name only". Tensions continued to rise in the MDC-T as Tsvangirai loyalists called for Mangoma to be punished. On 15 February, Mangoma was reportedly assaulted at the MDC-T headquarters in the presence of Tsvangirai. On 7 March, the MDC-T National Council suspended Mangoma as deputy treasurer general pending his appearance before an Independent Disciplinary Tribunal in accordance with the party constitution. On the same day, party secretary-general Tendai Biti, believed to be among the sponsors of the anti-Tsvangirai movement, quickly dismissed the controversial decision as null and void, arguing that due process had not been followed in line with the party constitution. On 16 February, MDC-T bigwigs boycotted a Tsvangirai rally in Harare. They included Biti, Mangoma, youth assembly chairperson Solomon Madzore, youth secretary-general Promise Mkwananzi, and Harare provincial chairman Paul Madzore. On 26 April, the Biti faction, now calling itself the *Renewal Team*, announced Tsvangirai's suspension from the party by the MDC-T National Council, accusing him of a "remarkable failure of leadership" and of transforming the party "into a fiefdom of the leader". In turn, on 29 April, Tsvangirai announced the expulsion of Biti, along with eight other members. Tsvangirai accused Biti of being an 'opportunist' who was being manipulated by ZANU-PF.

The *power struggle in the* MDC-T dragged the courts into its wrangles. On 27 June, in response to a case brought by the Tsvangirai faction, the High Court barred the Renewal Team from passing any resolutions on the party's behalf before the courts had sat to resolve the power struggle. In defiance of the court ruling, on 29 June, Biti and his Renewal Team announced the expulsion of Tsvangirai for alleged misconduct. The wrangles continued throughout the year with each faction claiming they were the genuine MDC. The Tsvangirai faction had control of most of the party's assets, including the party headquarters and the majority of the legislators elected on the MDC-T ticket, although a number of the parliamentarians backed Biti's faction. Tsvangirai also had the grassroots support in urban areas.

The two MDC breakaway formations took steps to unite. On 26 November, Biti's Renewal Team and Welshman Ncube's MDC-N officially signed a unity pact, coming together under a new movement dubbed the *Democratic Union.* Biti announced that the two formations had carried out the first part of the reunification exercise. There was widespread scepticism about the new party's chances of success. Biti's group did not appear to have grassroots support, while Ncube's party had performed dismally in the 2013 election, in which it had failed to win even a single seat and had gained a presence in parliament only through proportional representation.

Although they celebrated the power wrangles in the opposition, ZANU-PF *infighting* almost tore that party apart too. The two factions, led by Vice President Joice Mujuru and Justice Minister Emmerson Mnangagwa, continued to jostle for supremacy, battling relentlessly to succeed President Robert Mugabe. For most of the year, Mujuru appeared to have the upper hand; her faction had trounced Mnangagwa's in the party's provincial elections at the end of 2013, with figures loyal to Mujuru winning control of nine out of ZANU-PF's ten provinces. This was a significant victory for her. According to the then party constitution, provincial chairpersons and their executives played a central role in electing the party's national chairperson, two vice-presidents, and future presidential nominee.

In what looked like a boost to the Mujuru faction and the *downfall of Information Minister Jonathan Moyo*, on 6 June Mugabe described Moyo as "the devil incarnate", accusing him of appointing people who were sympathetic to the opposition as editors of state-owned newspapers. This was interpreted as an attack on the Mnangagwa faction, as Moyo was a known Mnangagwa ally. On 7 June, at the funeral of party stalwart Nathan Shamuyarira, Mugabe accused Moyo of fomenting divisions within the party. In a clear reference to Moyo, he described divisive elements in ZANU-PF as "weevils in our midst". Mujuru appeared on course to win the succession battle. Buoyed by the attack, ZANU-PF Secretary for Administration, Didymus Mutasa, a staunch Mujuru ally and Mugabe confidante, indicated that the party would "treat weevils by spraying Gamatox [a powerful pesticide] and they will all die".

Mujuru's attack on the media following *revelations of corruption* – which implicated a number of people aligned or sympathetic to her faction – did not help her. Early in the year, in what was seen as an extension of ZANU-PF's factional wars, the media exposed massive salary scandals in public institutions, including the national broadcaster. The state-controlled media played a significant part in this exposure. As acting president, Mujuru told a meeting on 8 February that detractors were behind the exposure. She said the corruption scandals should not be discussed in the media but should be handled by the Office of the President. Observers interpreted this as an attempt to gag the media and the intervention was widely condemned, with the MDC-T calling for Mujuru to resign for condoning corruption. This might have signalled the beginning of the dramatic weakening of the Mujuru faction. In defiance of Mujuru, on 20 February, Moyo urged both private and public media to intensify efforts to expose corruption, indicating that corruption was "the biggest vice that threatens national interest".

The Mujuru faction's fortunes took a further dive during the chaotic *elective conference of the* ZANU-PF *youth league*, held in August. Revelations on 8 August that delegates had gone to bed hungry prompted Mugabe's family to intervene by providing food. The fact that the person charged with fundraising for the event was the Mujuru loyalist Mutasa, did not augur well for the Mujuru faction. In his conference speech on the same day, Mugabe accused Mutasa of destroying the party, claiming that he had failed to mobilise resources as he concentrated on manoeuvring to secure power at the forthcoming ZANU-PF elective congress at the expense of the party. Mugabe revealed that his party was broke, saying thousands of party supporters attending the conference were facing transportation and accommodation challenges, while also going for the whole day on empty stomachs. The conference descended into chaos when voting took place, with accusations of irregularities and outright vote rigging and kidnappings. Rival factions squabbled over the choice of leaders, which resulted in a secret ballot. The accusations of impropriety were repeated by Mugabe on 14 August. He said he was embarrassed by the way senior officials had interfered with the operations of the youth league to the extent of coercing them to choose a leader they had never liked. The Mujuru faction, which emerged as the winner in the chaotic voting, was the target of the accusations. Unsurprisingly, there were claims that Mutasa was biased against the Mnangagwa faction.

The second half of the year witnessed the *political rise of Mrs Mugabe,* which culminated in the decapitation of the Mujuru faction. Oppah Muchinguri, the then women's affairs secretary, played a pivotal role. In July, it was announced that she was to relinquish her post in favour of Grace Mugabe, the president's wife. Speaking to a provincial paper on 1 August, Muchinguri launched a thinly veiled attack on Mujuru, suggesting she was impatient for President Mugabe to step down. On 5 August, at the youth conference, Muchinguri claimed the party was succumbing to factionalism, urging the youth to desist from divisive tendencies and rally behind Mugabe and his wife. Following the announcement that Muchinguri was to make way for her in the Women's League, Mrs Mugabe embarked on a series of 'Meet the People' rallies and 'Thank You' rallies, which took her to all provinces of the country. It was at these rallies that she unleashed vicious attacks on Mujuru and her allies, accusing her, among other things, of corruption and plotting to unseat Mugabe. She called on Mujuru to resign. At one of the rallies, Mrs Mugabe revealed that she had ordered her husband to "baby dump" his deputy. On 15 August, as expected, the *Women's League conference* in Harare endorsed the nomination of Mrs Mugabe as the sole candidate for the position of Women's League national secretary. This heralded her entry into active politics, adding what commentators indicated would be another dimension to the ZANU-PF succession battles. Observers saw Mrs Mugabe's elevation as a ploy by the Mnangagwa faction to neutralise Mujuru. On 9 October, Muchinguri confirmed this observation when she revealed that Mrs Mugabe's ascendency was a well-thought-out and calculated plot to stop political rivals from gaining ground in the ZANU-PF succession struggles. She pointed out that the plan was designed to scuttle Mujuru's bid for the presidency. In September, Mrs Mugabe controversially graduated from the *University of Zimbabwe* with a PhD in sociology, fuelling speculation that the award was meant to strengthen her credentials for political office. The doctorate torched a controversy. There were protests and speculation, with critics insisting that the doctorate had not been earned, but was a political conferment by a university where her husband is the chancellor. Rumours circulated that this was a 'super-speedy' PhD, completed in two months. Joining the chorus of condemnation – with some urging the return of the degree – the Zimbabwe National Students Union (ZNSU) announced that they would take President Mugabe to court over the awarding of the controversial doctorate to his wife. Unsurprisingly, ZANU-PF and the state media strongly defended the award. Instead of referring to Mrs Mugabe as 'Amai' (Mother), they began referring to her as 'Doctor Amai'.

Mrs Mugabe's elevation was confirmed at the party's elective congress in December. Contrary to widely held perceptions that she was a tool of the Mnangagwa faction, it later emerged that she might have presidential ambitions of her own. On 3 October, she said she had "so much ambition", a statement that was widely interpreted as signalling her presidential aspirations. Mrs Mugabe's attacks on Mujuru acted as a catalyst for the *decimation of the Mujuru faction*. By the time the congress was held, many of the Mujuru-aligned party chairpersons had been suspended or paralysed. They included Ray Kaukonde, the hitherto powerful chairperson of Mashonaland East province. He was accused of being the main funder of the Mujuru faction and was removed on 10 November, bringing to six the number of provincial chairpersons suspended in the run-up to the congress. The culling of Mujuru loyalists was extended to other party stalwarts. On 13 November, ZANU-PF expelled war veterans' leader Jabulani Sibanda and suspended party spokesperson Rugare Gumbo, who was finally expelled by the party's central committee on 3 December. On the same day, in a move seen as designed to further weaken the Mujuru faction, the central committee endorsed amendments to the party's constitution and nominees to the central committee. The amendment allowed Mugabe to directly appoint his deputies, giving him sole power to anoint his successor. As the congress approached, Mujuru faction bigwigs continued to fall. On 24 November, Mutasa lost his seat on the central committee following defeat in the party elections. On 25 November, Mujuru lost her bid to secure a central committee post after her district of origin, Mount Darwin, rejected her application. In other elections, a number of other senior party members linked to her faction failed to make it. Among the politburo members who suffered the same fate were cabinet ministers Dzikamai Mavhaire, Francis Nhema, Flora Buka, Tendai Savanhu and Simbarashe Mumbengegwi. By the time the ZANU-PF Sixth National People's Congress began on 2 December, the Mujuru faction had been effectively neutralised.

The ZANU-PF *elective congress* (Harare, 2–7 December) confirmed the fall of the Mujuru camp and the rise and triumph of the Mnangagwa faction. Mujuru and her senior loyalists, notably Mutasa and Gumbo, did not attend. Mnangagwa was appointed as vice president of the party and Mrs Mugabe was confirmed as the Women's League boss, which automatically propelled her onto the party's politburo. Mugabe criticised Mujuru in his closing remarks on 7 December. Reflecting the complexity of the balancing game in ZANU-PF, he closed the congress without announcing who his deputies would be. Indicating that he would not be rushed, he promised to announce the politburo and presidium the following week. This delay was a violation of the party's constitution, which requires him to appoint politburo members and members of the presidium during the sitting of congress.

On 10 December, Mugabe finally announced the *politburo and presidium*. As expected, Mujuru and her loyalists were sidelined. The positions of vice president and second secretary of the party were handed to Emmerson Mnangagwa and the little-known diplomat Phekezela Mphoko. In contrast to the previous arrangement, in which the president, his two deputies, secretary for administration and national chairperson constituted the presidium, the presidium now comprised only the president and his two deputies. A *cabinet reshuffle* was announced on 11 December, when Mugabe replaced Mujuru, seven ministers and a deputy minister who had been fired earlier. Mnangagwa and Mphoko were, as expected, appointed as the two vice presidents. The former would continue as minister of justice, legal and parliamentary affairs, while the latter took over the national healing, peace and reconciliation portfolio.

There were no significant changes in *human rights, democracy and the rule of law*. The police continued to be criticised as a partial force serving ZANU-PF. On 29 January, police arrested five NGO activists for participating in a demonstration in Chitungwiza. They were released without charge. On 27 February, police arrested 12 leaders of the ZNSU during a demonstration against poor education standards at Harare Polytechnic. They were reportedly beaten in police custody. On 13 February, police violently broke up a march by Women of Zimbabwe members who intended to petition parliament over the deteriorating national economic situation. In Victoria Falls, on June 28, four members of the Bulawayo Agenda were arrested and detained on charges of contravening the Public Order and Security Act (POSA). When the case went to court, they were acquitted. On 14 July, the little known Transform Zimbabwe political party leader Jacob Ngarivhume and 13 party supporters were arrested and detained at the Gweru Central Police Station on charges of breaching POSA. Ngarivhume was acquitted in court.

Foreign Affairs

As in previous years, relations with most African and Asian countries and organisations remained largely friendly. There was some movement in the strained relations with the OECD countries, but little real change. ZANU-PF continued blaming the country's woes on 'illegal' Western sanctions.

SADC as a block remained steadfast in its support of Mugabe. After the 2013 elections, SADC's mediation role in Zimbabwe ended and so Zimbabwe was no longer a constant item on the agenda for SADC meetings. However, Tsvangirai still approached SADC with grievances. On 18 August, he wrote to SADC indicating that Zimbabwe needed an urgent return to legitimacy and calling for fresh polls. SADC ignored him. On 19 November, he expressed disgust at the conduct of South Africa following the release of a damning report on the 2002 presidential elections in Zimbabwe. He accused South Africa and SADC of turning a blind eye to atrocities in Zimbabwe. Like SADC, the AU continued to stand by Mugabe. On 1 February, the AU summit took the position that African leaders would not attend the EU-Africa Summit scheduled for April in Belgium if the EU did not invite Mugabe. When his wife was denied a visa, Mugabe boycotted the summit. Zimbabwe remained active in continental ventures.

In August, Zimbabwe was a party to the Algiers Declaration on the establishment of the African Mechanism for Police Cooperation (AFRIPOL).

Mugabe's stature in Africa seemed to rise. On 30 January, the AU summit officially opened in Addis Ababa (Ethiopia) and Mugabe was elected first vice chair of the AU Bureau, a supreme organ of the AU tasked with steering the organisation's agenda with the assistance of the AU Commission. Mugabe represented Southern Africa in his new post. In August, he took over as chair of SADC at the two-day SADC Heads of State and Government Summit in Victoria Falls, which began on 17 August.

Good relations with *China* continued, but there were signs that China was not going to give Zimbabwe a blank cheque. In August, Mugabe went to China on a week-long state visit. The two countries signed several deals, mostly in the area of infrastructure development, but details remained sketchy. It later emerged that China had made no commitment to providing budgetary support and Finance Minister Patrick Chinamasa asserted that Zimbabwe was not seeking any. On 25 August, Chinamasa signed a 'securitisation framework' with the China Export and Credit Insurance Corporation (Sinosure) for various projects for which Zimbabwe was seeking funding. In a sign that Beijing was tightening its lending terms and expected debtors to be more accountable, Chinamasa reported on 10 September that Zimbabwe had to pay $ 180 m in Chinese loan repayments or face losing its credit line.

Zimbabwe's relations with its traditional ally *Russia* remained good. Russian investors stepped up their presence in Zimbabwe, competing with China for a share of the country's rich resources, including platinum, diamonds, commodities and a bank. On 5 June a Russian daily reported that a Russian consortium of Russian Vi Holding, Rostec and Vnesheconombank had announced that they planned a $ 3 bn investment to build Zimbabwe's largest platinum mine.

Zimbabwe continued to cooperate with *Iran*. In September, Minister of Small and Medium Enterprises Sithembiso Nyoni underlined Iran's progress in various industrial spheres. She said Zimbabwe would import quality medicines and medical equipment from Iran. Nyoni held a meeting with Iranian Minister of Cooperatives, Labour and Social Welfare Ali Rabiyee and they discussed the expansion of cooperation.

Relations with the EU thawed a little. In what it said were measures to encourage reform, the EU suspended targeted sanctions against eight Zimbabwean government officials on 17 February, but maintained the restrictive measures against Mugabe and his wife. However, Zimbabwe's head of delegation to the African-Caribbean-Pacific and EU Joint Parliamentary Assembly said any claims made by the EU that it would lift standing travel bans were incorrect because of the need for economic reform. On 30 October, the EU announced the lifting of its 12-year suspension of direct financial aid to the government of Zimbabwe. This was seen as a major step towards the normalisation of the frosty EU-Zimbabwe relations. The EU also announced that from 2015 it would start a € 234 m five-year funding programme to support health, agriculture and governance initiatives.

There was little improvement in *relations with the* USA. On 5–6 August, US President Barack Obama hosted the US-Africa Leaders Summit in an effort to strengthen American ties with the continent. Mugabe was excluded because he was still a Specially Designated National and was not on the list of invited heads of state released on 23 January. Mugabe's spokesperson, George Charamba, dismissed Obama's decision to snub Mugabe as an indication that the summit was not about the USA and Africa, but about the USA and certain African countries. The USA maintained targeted sanctions on 113 Zimbabwean individuals and 70 entities – mostly farms and legal entities owned by the targeted individuals. During the year, two US citizens were prosecuted in the Federal District Court in Chicago for engaging in "public relations, political consulting and lobbying" US officials to lift sanctions against Mugabe and Zimbabweans on the targeted sanctions list in exchange for payment.

Relations with *multilateral organisations* changed little. On 10 January, the IMF announced that its management had approved a request for a six-month extension of the Staff Monitored Program to allow time for Zimbabwe to strengthen its policies and deliver on outstanding commitments under the programme. On 27 March, it said it would shortly be resuming its resident representative office in Harare. The IMF had not had a resident representative in Zimbabwe for almost a decade. On 18 June, the IMF Executive Board concluded the Article IV consultation. Significantly, the report noted that Zimbabwe's economic rebound experienced since 2009 had ended. On 27 September, the IMF said it would not lend more money to Zimbabwe, because the country was in arrears with repayments of previous loans. The World Bank's lending programme also remained inactive due to arrears. The Bank's role was limited to technical assistance and analytical work. At the beginning of the year, Zimbabwe owed the IMF and the World Bank $ 124 m and $ 1 bn, respectively. In its outlook for 2013–15, the AfDB reported that its operations in Zimbabwe had been limited by the country's arrears situation. Nevertheless, the bank remained engaged through policy dialogue, technical assistance and capacity building, and knowledge and advisory services through the Fragile States Facility. It also supported infrastructure development in the water and energy sectors through the African Water Facility and management of the Zimbabwe Multi-Donor Trust Fund (Zim-Fund), as well as providing some support to the private sector.

Socioeconomic Developments

The IMF confirmed that the economic recovery enjoyed during the Government of National Unity years had ended, although *economic indicators* did not plunge. In many cases, this was rather a slow-down or slow decline. Reserve Bank of Zimbabwe figures showed that the December consumer price index stood at 99.5%, and the year-on-year price increase at –0.8%. According to Economist Intelligence Unit (EIU) estimates, real GDP growth was 3.0%. The EIU put the nominal GDP at $ 2.5 bn. The current account balance, excluding transfers, was –$ 1.045 bn, while total international reserves dropped to $ 448 m from $ 475 m in 2013. In the budget statement, the finance minister forecast that the public and publicly guaranteed debt burden would be $ 8.4 bn by December, comprising an external debt of $ 7.2 bn and a domestic debt of $ 1.2 bn. The minister admitted that the country was in debt distress, characterised by large external payment arrears against a background of limited fiscal space and rising domestic debt. Zimbabwe's ability to mobilise resources to finance its economic strategy (ZIMASSET) was therefore compromised, "undermining the process of socio-economic development and poverty reduction". Zimbabwe performed poorly in a number of world *league tables*. It was ranked 171st out of 189 economies in Doing Business 2015 and the World Economic Forum's Global Competitiveness Report 2013–14 ranked Zimbabwe 131st out of 148 countries. The Human Development Index for 2013 was 0.492, which placed Zimbabwe 156th out of 187 countries – an improvement on 160th in 2012.

On the *humanitarian* front, the country faced a number of challenges. In late January and early February, heavy rains in parts of the country resulted in deaths and displacement of people, coupled with destruction of property. The worst affected areas were Chivi and Masvingo districts in Masvingo province and Tsholotsho district in Matabeleland North province. On 11 February, the government launched an international appeal for $ 20 m to help some 20,000 people displaced by the floods. According to ReliefWeb, by the end of February, an estimated 2,194 households had been moved to the Chingwizi resettlement camp. By May, the more than 15,625 people evacuated remained in dire living conditions. In February, the Ministry of Health and Child Care reported that at least 38 people had died as a result of *waterborne and related epidemics*, including diarrhoea and dysentery. There were 16 suspected new typhoid cases. At the end of February, a typhoid outbreak was reported in Harare's high-density suburb of Mabvuku, with at least nine cases confirmed. The suburb had gone for four months without water supplies. In July, a typhoid fever scare hit parts of Harare; 18 new suspected cases were recorded in one week.

In terms of *food security*, according to WFP estimates released in July, the country would have a cereal harvest surplus of 253,174 tonnes from a total cereal harvest of 1,680,293 tonnes. The proportion of households with an acceptable food consumption score increased to 68%. The number of people estimated to be food insecure for the 2014/15 consumption year was estimated to be 565,000, representing 6% of the rural population. This was a decrease from 2013 figures. Projections by the Commercial Farmers Union put total agricultural production at 2.5 m tonnes up from 1.6 m tonnes in 2008 at the height of the economic problems. However, according to EIU figures, the production of wheat, sugar and soya beans showed a marked decline compared with 2000, before the controversial land reform programme was launched. Tea was the only crop that saw an increase. Production of the staple crop, maize, was still less than half the output in 2000.

On *demographic indicators*, according to 2014 estimates, the death rate stood at 10.6 deaths per 1,000 people. The net migration rate was estimated at 21.8 migrants per 1,000 people. The flow of Zimbabweans into South Africa and Botswana in search of better economic opportunities did not show signs of abating. Average life expectancy for the total population was 55.7 years, while the infant mortality rate was estimated at 26.6 deaths per 1,000 live births. Rankings published by the 'African Economist' magazine in June showed Zimbabwe leading the literacy rate in Africa, coming in at 91%, despite a decade-long economic crisis that had impacted negatively on the quality of education.

Progress was reported in the country's response to the HIV/AIDS scourge. According to the Zimbabwe AIDS Response Progress Report 2014 (for 2013), about 46,000 deaths had been averted by antiretroviral therapy (ART), with infections averted by prevention of mother-to-child transmission (PMTCT) totalling 15,000. A combined total of 324,000 life years were gained by ART and PMTCT. The HIV incidence rate was 0.98, compared with 1.25 the previous year. There were 61,476 HIV-related deaths during the year, down from 87,335 in 2012. HIV prevalence among pregnant women aged 15–24 was 9.9% compared with 11.6% in 2012.

The education and health delivery systems continued to experience problems of staffing, equipment and funding, and health and educational personnel contributed significantly to the brain drain. Industrial actions and threats of industrial action arising out of salary disputes were a constant feature throughout the year, further compromising these sectors. At the beginning of the year, the Progressive Teachers' Union of Zimbabwe (PTUZ) said its members would go on strike when schools opened the following week if the much-awaited salary negotiations with the government failed to yield positive results. There were still problems by the end of the year. On 23 December, the PTUZ was again threatening to strike following the government's failure to pay annual bonuses. In October, about 300 junior doctors went on strike when the government failed to meet their ultimatum to address their demands for a pay rise from $ 283 to $ 1,200 a month. In addition to industrial unrest, *workforce redundancies* hit the economy. They were a major issue that exacerbated Zimbabwe's already high unemployment rate. According to the Retrenchment Board, some 1,300 people were made redundant in the first quarter alone. Significantly, manufacturing laid off 550 workers and services 200. Company closures, low levels of FDI and liquidity problems were major contributory factors. The loss of jobs fuelled the informalisation of the economy and migration, mostly to other southern African countries, particularly South Africa and Botswana.

There appeared to be some movement in the controversial *indigenisation policy*, with reports of a major government climb-down in the state-owned 'Sunday Mail'. On 25 May, in an interview with

Jonathan Moyo, the newspaper reported that the Indigenisation Act would be amended and investors would be allowed to recover costs. In addition, a production-sharing model would be proposed. The paper interpreted this as a victory for former Reserve Bank governor, Gideon Gono, and moderates in the government. There was no let-up in the dismal performance of *parastatals and local authorities*. In addition to the massive corruption over salaries unearthed at state enterprises, parastatals such as Ziscosteel, National Railways of Zimbabwe, ZBC and Air Zimbabwe continued to perform badly, as did all local authorities. According to the 'Zimbabwe Independent' newspaper, the situation was attributable to, among other things, the sustained and systematic militarisation of parastatals, public enterprises and local authorities. This had contributed to breeding a culture of patronage, corruption and looting as these institutions were staffed mainly by people who did not have the requisite qualifications, experience or competence to run them efficiently and profitably.

On 27 November, Finance Minister Patrick Chinamasa presented the *2015 national budget* with the theme "Towards an Empowered Society and Inclusive Economic Growth". Chinamasa proposed a $ 4.1 bn budget. Like all previous budgets, its most notable feature was the dominance of civil servants' salaries. Of this budget, $ 3.3 bn, representing 81% of total expenditure, would go towards employment costs, leaving a balance of $ 798 m for operations, debt service and capital development programmes. The proposed allocation for the capital budget was $ 341 m, while that for operations and maintenance was $ 384 m. Chinamasa projected a GDP growth rate at market prices of 3.2% for 2015, admitting that such levels of growth remained inadequate for the country "to begin making a dent at the prevailing levels of capacity utilisation in the economy and high unemployment". Positive growth was projected in all sectors. Notably, manufacturing which had a growth rate of –4.9% was projected to grow by 1.7%. In contrast, the projected growth for agriculture, hunting and fishing was 3.4% down from 23.4%.

Zimbabwe in 2015

The year was dominated by factionalism in the Zimbabwe African National Union-Patriotic Front (ZANU-PF), with purges in the party becoming a regular occurrence. The intraparty fighting pitted the faction allegedly aligned with the president's wife against the camp loyal to one of the vice presidents. Relentless rumours about President Mugabe's health were a constant talking point throughout the year. As in previous years, much of Zimbabwe's foreign relations centred on controversies about 'illegal' western sanctions, an issue which again saw very little change in the positions of the key players. The economy showed signs of deterioration.

Domestic Politics

The year started with the fallout from the decimation of the *Mujuru faction.* Throughout the year, there were endless purges of perceived allies of ousted Vice President Joice Mujuru. On 14 January, the sacked political heavyweight, former ZANU-PF secretary for Administration and Presidential Affairs Minister *Didymus Mutasa,* issued a scathing press statement "on behalf of all the loyal members of ZANU-PF who are determined to restore the image of our party". The statement accused President Robert Mugabe and his wife of fanning hatred and division in the party. Mutasa described the congress that sacked him and other party members allegedly loyal to Mrs Mujuru as illegal, and the sackings as therefore null and void. He threatened legal action. Critics interpreted Mutasa's venomous statement as a case of sour grapes for his ouster. Quoting legal experts, state-controlled media ridiculed Mutasa's legal bid as "an exercise in futility", claiming that the planned application had no legal merit. In the face of attacks by his erstwhile colleagues, Mutasa continued his fight against his former party. On 30 January,

 | DOI:10.1163/9789004404335_009

he hinted that Mujuru would be filing a lawsuit against the president's wife, Grace Mugabe, over attacks that had led to the former's expulsion from the party. On 2 February, he said he would attend ZANU-PF's planned disciplinary hearing against him, out of his "enduring respect" for President Mugabe. The hearing had been delayed by Mrs Mugabe's absence. The disciplinary committee was led by Vice President Phelekezela Mphoko. Other committee members were secretary for Women's Affairs Grace Mugabe, ZANU-PF national commissar Saviour Kasukuwere, secretary for legal affairs Patrick Chinamasa, Secretary for Youth Pupurai Togarepi and politburo member Kembo Mohadi.

Unconfirmed reports of *Mugabe's poor health*, which were traditionally voiced at the beginning of the year, this time included his wife. On 22 January, Mugabe reported that she had undergone an appendectomy in Singapore. The following day, there were reports that Mugabe had undergone a major prostate cancer operation, also in Singapore, but this was denied by Mugabe's spokesperson, George Charamba, who said he had gone for "an annual review of his eyes". On his return, Mugabe did not mention his own operation, but disclosed that he and his family had undergone medical check-ups during their holiday. Rumours about Mrs Mugabe's health intensified with her continued absence from the country. On 9 February, the presidential spokesman denied reports that she was in a coma. In March, unconfirmed reports in the private media reported that she had received treatment for colon cancer. Amidst the reports and speculation about his wife, Mugabe's own health continued to be the subject of rumours, fuelled by his frequent trips to Singapore. After his return from annual leave in February, he had flown to the city-state three times by the end of April. Mrs Mugabe disappeared from public view and was not fulfilling her party obligations and other duties as head of the ZANU-PF Women's League, amid reports that she was ill. She was said to be seeking treatment abroad. On 3 June, she reappeared on the political scene and scoffed at reports of her poor health, insisting that she was as fit as a fiddle. *Mugabe's fall at the airport* escalated speculation on his health: on 4 February, on his arrival from Ethiopia, he missed a step and tumbled off the podium at Harare International Airport. The incident quickly became major news. According to reports, journalists at the scene were forced to delete pictures of the president lying on the ground. With videos of the fall going viral, the fallout from the incident lasted for some time, with government spin-doctors and detractors tussling over what actually happened. It was also reported that up to 27 members of the presidential security and advance team who stood by as Mugabe fell were suspended on 6 February. The opposition unsurprisingly capitalised on the event, using it as evidence to support their questioning Mugabe's fitness to rule.

Following the purging of Mujuru loyalists, *ZANU-PF factional fighting* took on a new dimension. By the second half of the year, it was being speculated that the alliance between Grace Mugabe and Vice President Emmerson Mnangagwa that had annihilated the Mujuru faction was unravelling. The increasingly influential Mrs Mugabe was said to be working with ZANU-PF's ambitious Young Turks, known as Generation 40 (G40). As in previous years, the factional wars were associated with ZANU-PF's fractious succession politics. There was speculation that rather than helping Mnangagwa become president, Mrs Mugabe was preparing herself for the position. Phelekezela Mphoko, the other vice president, was reported to be in the Grace Mugabe camp. On 8 August, President Mugabe denied for the first time speculation that he was lining up his wife to succeed him. The factional fighting pitted two formations against each other: the Mnangagwa-aligned 'Team Lacoste' and the Grace Mugabe-aligned G40. The most vocal members of the G40 formation were Higher Education Minister Jonathan Moyo; party national commissar, Saviour Kasukuwere; and Mugabe's nephew, Patrick Zhuwao. They were openly opposed to Mnangagwa, viewing him as unfit to run the party and country.

One of the high-profile public battles between the factions involved choosing a candidate for the *Harare East constituency*. The factions picked rival candidates and the case went all the way to the High Court. On 6 May, the court ruled that both candidates could contest the 10 June election. On 16 May, it was reported that the G40 faction had upstaged Mnangagwa's camp in the battle for the constituency. ZANU-PF officially chose G40's preferred candidate, Terence Mukupe, to represent the party over Mnangagwa loyalist Mavis Gumbo. Mnangagwa's woes were not helped by his political gaffes. In an interview with 'New Africa' magazine in September, he described the immensely popular late vice president Joshua Nkomo as a sell-out. This damaged Mnangagwa's image and presidential ambitions because it alienated Ndebele people both within and outside the ruling party. As the factional fighting intensified, the Mnangagwa camp reportedly tried to outflank the G40 when, on 12 November, it was reported that the *Masvingo provincial executive* was planning to be the first to endorse Mnangagwa as Mugabe's official number two ahead of the party's December conference. This was apparently in response to the G40's strategy to oust Mnangagwa. In October, the G40 were reported to be plotting to push for a constitutional amendment to re-introduce a clause that would compel ZANU-PF to have a woman in the party presidium. What fuelled speculation that this was targeted at Mnangagwa was the fact that Mphoko, the other vice president, appeared to be safe as his appointment was in accordance with the 1987 ZANU-ZAPU Unity Accord. The G40 appeared to have secured the support of two influential organs of the party: the Youth League and the Women's League, headed by Grace Mugabe.

The drama in the *factions of the MDC* (Movement for Democratic Change) spilled over into 2015. On 17 March, 17 opposition MPs and four senators were expelled from parliament by order of the Speaker of Parliament, Jacob Mudenda, after they broke away to form a new party. The 21 had been elected or nominated on MDC-T (Tsvangirai) tickets. They later split to form MDC Renewal, led by former finance minister Tendai Biti. As 14 of the MPs had been directly elected in the 2013 election, the expulsions triggered by-elections in their constituencies. The MDC-T would be able to appoint replacements for the other seven seats, which were allocated according to the proportion of votes cast in the 2013 election. Also on 17 March, Biti responded by vowing to challenge the expulsion in court, although his legal challenge would be unlikely to succeed. Biti also made allegations that MDC-T was working with ZANU-PF to destroy his MDC Renewal. This was hardly a believable allegation, given the tensions between MDC-T and ZANU-PF.

In a *series of by-elections* triggered by the expulsion of the MPs and senators, deaths of legislators, and the elevation of Mnangagwa to the vice presidency, ZANU-PF secured easy victories, beginning on 28 March, when it won Chirumhanzu-Zibangwe and Mount Darwin constituencies. On 10 June, ZANU-PF won all 16 contested seats in parliamentary by-elections and, on 20 December, won in Nkulumane, thereby improving its political presence in Bulawayo. The MDC-T boycotted all the by-elections, vowing not to take part in any future elections before the alignment of the Electoral Act with the new Constitution. The minor parties that contested the by-elections lost by huge margins.

Throughout the year, there was intense speculation about ousted Vice President *Joice Mujuru's political intentions.* Her allies, Rugare Gumbo and Didymus Mutasa, had indicated that she was going to form her own political party and in April Mutasa claimed that efforts were underway to form a party to be called Zimbabwe People First (ZPF), with Mujuru as its leader. Mutasa insisted the party would be the 'original' ZANU-PF. For some time, Mujuru maintained her silence and all political statements were made by Mutasa and Gumbo. Finally, in September, Mujuru came into the open about her future and gave the strongest indication that she would challenge President Mugabe. On 8 September, she unveiled her party manifesto, entitled *Blueprint to Unlock Investment and Leverage for Development* (*BUILD*). She claimed that BUILD reflected her party's 'proposal to translate our vision for a better Zimbabwe into reality'.

In addition to economic issues, the manifesto contained other important provisions, including acknowledging dual citizenship and promoting and supporting press freedom. ZANU-PF loyalists ridiculed the manifesto, though it received favourable reviews from some commentators.

President Mugabe announced a *cabinet reshuffle* on 11 September, adding to the bloated cabinet. He appointed four new ministers and 10 deputies. Jonathan Moyo was moved to the Ministry of Higher and Tertiary Education from the Information, Media and Broadcasting Services Ministry, where he was replaced by Christopher Mushowe. Saviour Kasukuwere was moved to the Ministry of Local Government Public Works and National Housing, being replaced at the Water and Climate Ministry by Oppah Muchinguri. Ignatius Chombo was moved from the Local Government Ministry and re-assigned to the Ministry of Home Affairs. Nyasha Chikwinya was appointed to take the lead at the Ministry of Women's Affairs. There had been speculation that Mugabe would bring his wife into the cabinet, to take over the Women's Affairs Ministry. Mugabe's nephew, Patrick Zhuwao was named minister of youth development, indigenisation and economic empowerment.

ZANU-PF's 15th Annual National People's Conference opened on 11 December in Victoria Falls. As expected, the party's factional in-fighting escalated, with accusations and counter-accusations of plots between the two camps. So vicious were the conflicts that Mugabe openly admitted that factionalists were "threatening to tear each other apart at this conference". There were reports that the G40 was trying to force Mnangagwa out of the race for the presidency by demoting him and replacing him in the presidium with Grace Mugabe. The influential Women's League had demanded in its resolutions to the conference that a woman be incorporated into the presidium by 2016. However, on 12 December, President Mugabe, in his closing speech, seemed to scuttle the plot by dismissing any plans of leadership change as 'dreams'. It is believed Mugabe saved Team Lacoste. In a departure from the norm, the conference ended on 12 December with no announcement of final resolutions. This was seen as an indication of the bruising factional in-fighting that had characterised ZANU-PF's succession politics throughout the year. Another significant development at the conference was the call by some delegates for a return to the Zimbabwe dollar.

Partly because of the factional conflicts in ZANU-PF, the *human rights situation* remained relatively stable during much of the year. However, there were reports that the government continued to violate human rights in defiance of protections enshrined in the new Constitution. According to HRW, the expected legislative framework and new or amended laws to improve human rights in line with the Constitution did not materialise. The organisation reported that police violated basic rights, such as freedom of expression and assembly, "using old laws that are inconsistent with the new constitution". Later in the year, there was some progress in the harmonisation of some pieces of legislation with the Constitution. According to the Zimbabwe Human Rights NGO Forum, by the end of the year the General Laws Amendment Bill of 2015 had addressed 125 Acts of Parliament and 51 Acts had been amended under the National Prosecuting Authority Act. An outstanding 116 Acts still required minor amendments, while 49 required substantial amendments.

Police harassment continued. Human rights activists faced severe restrictions on their work. Police frequently applied draconian laws such as the Public Order and Security Act and the Access to Information and Protection of Privacy Act to ban public meetings and gatherings. Journalists and opposition and other activists were prosecuted under these laws. Between October and December, the Zimbabwe Human Rights NGO Forum reported a cumulative total of 998 human rights violations. On 9 March, five armed men abducted 36-year-old journalist *Itai Dzamara*, a human rights activist, vocal Mugabe critic and leader of a protest group known as Occupy Africa Unity Square. At year's end, he had still not been found. The authorities consistently denied any government involvement. On

13 March, Dzamara's wife approached the High Court to compel the state to search for her husband. Judge David Mangota ordered the home affairs minister, the police commissioner-general and the director-general of the Central Intelligence Organization "to do all things necessary to determine Dzamara's whereabouts". The judge ordered the government to report to the court every two weeks on its progress with the case until Dzamara was found. They did not comply with the order.

There were violations of *freedoms of assembly and expression*. On 25 April, activists organised a car procession to raise awareness about Dzamara's disappearance. Police arrested 11 of the activists and detained them for six hours. They were released without charge. On 8 November, Highfield East MP Erick Murayi (MDC-T) and 16 others were arrested on charges of public violence and for holding a rally without police clearance. On the *press freedom* front, on 2 November police arrested three state media journalists who had published a report implicating senior police officers and Parks and Wildlife Authority rangers in the killing of elephants in Hwange National Park. On 12 November, the journalist Andrison Manyere was arrested in Harare for covering a demonstration by MDC-T activists against what they saw as reluctance by the Zimbabwe Electoral Commission to implement electoral reforms. He was later released without charge.

Foreign Affairs

With no major change in the country's domestic and foreign policy, there was little change in foreign relations. Relations with most African and Asian countries and organisations continued to be friendly. Relations with the OECD countries experienced some slight shifts. As had become the norm, ZANU-PF and the government blamed the country's deteriorating economic situation on 'illegal' western sanctions.

President Mugabe began the year as *Chairman of SADC*, a position he had assumed in August 2014. This role continued to be celebrated among his supporters and was used as an indication of his stature as a statesman. During his watch as SADC chairman, the *crisis in Lesotho* arose following the killing of the army commander in June. Mugabe expressed concern and worked to resolve the situation. His bid to diffuse the crisis included meetings with South Africa's Defence Minister Nosiviwe Mapisa-Nqakula, President Jacob Zuma's special envoy, in Harare on 30 June. As chairman of the bloc, Mugabe travelled extensively to countries in the region. This generated controversy with the opposition and critics complained about what they asserted was a waste of resources. In August, Mugabe handed over the SADC chairmanship to President Ian Khama of Botswana. While critics dismissed Mugabe's chairmanship as a non-event, his supporters defended his legacy at the helm of the organisation and the benefits to the country's international standing. Ironically, despite having its leader as chairman of SADC, Zimbabwe failed to pay its $ 2 m contribution for the year. Officials blamed the banking system, claiming that banks were "reluctant to conduct transactions from the country".

On 30 January, President Mugabe was appointed as the new *chairman of the AU*. While his supporters predictably celebrated, Mugabe's appointment drew criticism from Zimbabwean opposition parties and Mugabe critics. The MDC-T argued that he lacked "the political legitimacy to lead an Africa that should be looking to consolidate democracy and good governance", while the head of the ICG pointed out that the "elevation sends a negative signal of African solidarity with leaders who've misruled their countries". As was the case with his chairmanship of the SADC, Mugabe's tenure at the AU drew mixed review. His supporters hailed it as a success: the state-owned 'Sunday Mail' newspaper said that he had introduced processes and implemented plans that helped steer the AU into its current form. Critics, dismissed his tenure as a disaster, with 'The Zimbabwean' newspaper describing Mugabe as the AU's weakest leader in history. As head of the AU, Mugabe travelled extensively. During March, he made five trips to other African countries. Predictably, this brought criticism from people who saw it as a waste of money that the country could ill afford. Mugabe also faced harsh *criticism from abroad.* On 29 May, journalists confronted him during the inauguration of Nigerian President Muhammadu Buhari in Abuja and questioned him about his long stay in power. His supporters did not take kindly to this embarrassing encounter and the state media went into overdrive to denigrate the journalists.

While relations with most of Africa were good, the same could not be said of Zimbabwe's relations with *Botswana.* On 17 August, when Botswana's President Ian Khama took over as SADC chairman, he said he wanted the region "to be a beacon for democracy for Africa", and blasted "leaders who cling to power". Such were the relations between the two countries that observers interpreted the remarks as being directed at Zimbabwe. Relations with *South Africa* remained good. In April, President Mugabe paid his first state visit to South Africa since 1994 and the two countries strengthened bilateral relations with the signing of five agreements on 8 April. The agreements comprised the establishment of a binational commission to be led by the two heads of state; a memorandum of understanding on diplomatic consultations; a memorandum of understanding on trade cooperation; an agreement on mutual assistance between customs administrations; and an agreement on cooperation on water resources management.

On the international stage, Zimbabwe maintained good relations with *China.* On 1 December, China's President Xi Jinping arrived in Zimbabwe. He was easily the most prominent global leader to visit the country in many years. In an article in the state-controlled 'Herald' newspaper, Mr Xi said the two nations had a "deep and firm" friendship. On 22 December, Zimbabwe announced that the yuan would become the latest currency to be approved for public transactions in Zimbabwe. This was seen as part of the country's plans to increase trade with China. The decision was made following Beijing's confirmation that it would cancel $ 40 m of debts.

Zimbabwe strengthened relations with *Russia*, one of its traditional allies. On 4 January, state media reported that a high-powered Russian delegation would visit Zimbabwe that month to finalise some multi-million dollar projects aimed at improving water infrastructure in Harare and surrounding towns. They were aimed at dam construction, irrigation development and water management. In May, it was reported that Russian investors would be financing a $ 4 bn platinum mine in the Great Dyke. The investors said they would also carry out exploration for other minerals, which could add to their investment. This was in line with a 'roadmap' agreed in September 2014 during the visit of Russian Foreign Minister Sergei Lavrov.

Outside its circle of traditional allies and friends, Zimbabwe forged relations with *Belarus*. The two countries stepped up cooperation in sectors ranging from agriculture to mining. On 18 November, Mugabe approved a number of investment deals after his meeting with the visiting Viktor Sheiman, President Lukashenko's chief property manager. The deals covered agriculture, mining and agricultural equipment. Mugabe and Sheiman also discussed cooperation in electricity, road and bridge construction, housing and education.

There was no major shift in *relations with the EU*. The thaw continued, with the EU announcing a resumption of aid to Zimbabwe. On 16 February, the EU unveiled a $ 270 m aid package to support Zimbabwe's agriculture and health sectors. This marked the resumption of direct funding after more than ten years. However, the EU maintained its asset freeze and a travel ban on Mugabe and his wife, as well as an arms embargo. During the signing ceremony, EU Ambassador to Zimbabwe Philippe Van Damme cautioned that this move did not "mean that everything is suddenly sorted out and that we are entering a new honeymoon", pointing out that, although some obstacles had been cleared in the EU-Zimbabwe partnership, "new problems may emerge, old problems may reappear".

Zimbabwe's relations with the *UK* saw some activity. On 12 February, a UK private sector-led International Investor Delegation arrived in Zimbabwe to explore investment opportunities. The British Embassy claimed this signalled "the strengthening of business ties between the two countries". In March, DFID launched a programme to increase incomes and reduce poverty among smallholder farming households in chronically food and nutrition insecure districts and, on 7 September, approved new funding to support Zimbabwe's education sector. On 17 September, UK Foreign and Commonwealth Office Head of Central and Southern Africa Department Danae Dholakia, who was visiting Zimbabwe, met Minister of Water, Environment and Climate Oppah Muchinguri-Kashiri. According to the British Embassy in Harare, the two discussed, among other things, combating the illegal trade in wildlife; the UK's ongoing support to the water sector in Zimbabwe; and mitigating the impacts of global climate change on Zimbabwe in the context of the 21st Conference of Parties in Paris.

Relations with the US remained frosty. This became clear on 13 March, when two visiting US diplomats ruled out a change of policy with Zimbabwe. Speaking to reporters in Harare, Deputy Assistant Secretary of State for African Affairs Shannon Smith said the US would not relax travel bans and other sanctions against President Mugabe and his leadership during the year. However, on 3 July, speaking at the 239th US Independence Day anniversary in Harare, US Ambassador to Zimbabwe Bruce Wharton said his government was committed to the development of Zimbabwe and had embarked on various projects mutually beneficial to both countries. In a move that did not help bilateral relations, Mugabe was excluded from an AU meeting in July 2015 after he was snubbed by US President Barack Obama. Despite being the AU chairman, Mugabe was not among the leaders who met Obama at the AU headquarters in Addis Ababa (Ethiopia) on 28 July. Mugabe's spokesman said Mugabe was unmoved by Obama's visit to the AU and dismissed the event as like "a visit by any other visitor".

Relations with multilateral organisations were mixed. On 8 April, the management of the *IMF* completed the first review under the Staff-Monitored Program (SMP) with Zimbabwe. The IMF described the SMP as the "lynchpin of the authorities' roadmap for building a strong track record towards normalizing the relationship with Zimbabwe's creditors and mobilizing development partners' support". According to the IMF, the main objective of the programme was to strengthen Zimbabwe's external position as a prerequisite towards arrears clearance, normalisation of debt servicing, and restoring access to external financing. In September, the IMF indicated that, even if Zimbabwe undertook economic reforms, it would take at least three years before it could expect loans from international lenders. Zimbabwe stepped up its reengagement with creditors by, among other things, increasing payments to the *World Bank* and the *AfDB.* On 19 May, the World Bank urged Zimbabwe to urgently clear its arrears with the Bretton Woods Institutions and the AfDB in order to access the extra lines of credit necessary to fund the economy. The executive director of the World Bank's Africa Group, Louis Rene Peter Larose, pointed out that the resolution of Zimbabwe's debt overhang and the clearance of arrears needed "to be treated with the urgency it deserves".

Socioeconomic Developments

Zimbabwe faced some significant economic challenges during the year. *Economic indicators* reflected the challenges in the economy. Confirming signs of deflationary pressures, Reserve Bank of Zimbabwe figures showed that the December consumer price index was 98%. The year-on-year price increase was –2.4% compared with –0.2% in 2014. According to Economist Intelligence Unit (EIU) estimates, the real GDP growth was 0.2%, a sharp drop from 3.8% in 2014. The EIU put the nominal GDP at $ 13.9 bn, down from $ 14.2 bn. The current account balance was –$ 2.5 bn, up from –$ 1.0 bn, while total international reserves dropped to $ 297 m. In the budget statement, the finance minister estimated public and publicly guaranteed *debt burden* at $ 8.3 bn. The external debt consisted of debts of $ 1.4 bn. The arrears amounted to $ 5.4 bn, giving a total debt of $ 7.0 bn.

Zimbabwe performed poorly in a number of *world league tables.* In the World Bank's Doing Business 2016, the country was ranked 155th, down from 153rd in 2015 out of 189 economies. The World Economic Forum's Global Competitiveness Report 2014–15 ranked Zimbabwe 124th out of 144 countries. The Human Development Index for 2015 gave a figure of 0.509, which placed Zimbabwe 155th – an improvement from 156th in 2014.

On the humanitarian front, the country faced a number of challenges. In April, Masvingo Provincial Affairs Minister Shuvai Mahofa said the government would embark on the second relocation of nearly 3,000 Tokwe-Mukosi *flood victims* from the Nuanetsi Ranch to seven farms that had been identified for them in Mwenezi district. Each of the families would be allocated six hectares at the new plots. Another *cholera outbreak* hit the country. On 9 March, Health and Childcare Minister David Parirenyatwa announced that confirmed cholera cases had risen to 12, while three more suspected cases at Birchenough Bridge were still to be verified. By April, the situation appeared under control. Government and partners remained on alert following one new suspected cholera case in Manicaland Province and one suspected case in Mashonaland East Province.

Food security challenges resurfaced. According to the Vulnerability Assessment Committee (ZIMVAC) Report of 2015, maize production dropped by 49% from the average, with a likely cereal deficit of 650,000 tonnes. The crop production deficits were caused by poor rainfall distribution during the season. As a result 1.5 m people were at risk of food and livelihood insecurity. The ZIMVAC 2015 rural livelihoods assessment indicated that approximately 10% of the rural population were projected to be food-insecure for the period of

October–December and that 16% of the rural population were projected to be food-insecure for the period of January–March 2016.

According to *demographic indicators* produced by the World Bank, the death rate for the period 2011–15 stood at ten deaths per 1,000 of population. Due to the worsening economic situation, there was an increasing flow of Zimbabweans into South Africa and Botswana in search of better economic opportunities. UN estimates put the crude net migration rate at 4.35 migrants per 1,000 of population. Life expectancy for the total population was 51 years. The infant mortality rate was estimated at 47 deaths per 1000 live births (World Bank estimate). The literacy rate was a league-topping 91%, making Zimbabwe the leader in Africa.

According to the government, the *HIV/AIDS* epidemic remained "generalized, feminized and homogenous" and with continued declines in new infection rates, prevalence and AIDS-related mortality. UNAIDS figures showed that 1.6 m people were living with HIV. The prevalence rate among adults aged 15–49 was estimated at 16.7%. About 150,000 children aged 15 or under were living with HIV. Deaths due to AIDS were estimated at 39,000. There were 570,000 children aged 0–17 who had been orphaned by AIDS.

The *education and health* delivery systems continued to experience problems of staffing, equipment and funding. Health and education personnel remained a substantial part of the brain drain. Industrial action and threats of industrial action arising out of salary disputes were a constant feature throughout the year, further compromising these sectors. In September, teachers' unions threatened industrial action at the beginning of the third term. They wanted to force the government to address their concerns, which included working conditions and the withdrawal of salaries for more than 3,000 teachers found missing from their workstations during a human resources audit conducted by the Ministry of Primary and Secondary Education. On 27 December, government doctors gave their employer a five-day ultimatum to pay their December salaries and bonuses, threatening withdrawal of labour in the new year.

Job losses spiralled in the second half of the year as companies took advantage of a shock court ruling by the Supreme Court on 16 July that companies could lawfully terminate employees' contracts at any time without offering them packages, provided they had given them at least three months' notice. There was a flood of employment terminations as companies saw the termination of contracts on notice as a cost-effective way of firing workers without the need to give any explanation or conduct disciplinary hearings or take the costly retrenchment option. Figures for those who lost their jobs in July alone ranged from 20,000 to 25,000 in both private and state-run firms. Faced with the massive job losses, the government rushed to amend the labour laws. On 26 August, new labour regulations came into force that made it harder to retrench workers. Retrenchments could now only be allowed in specific circumstances, with a minimum retrenchment package of one month's pay for every two years of service. The regulations were backdated to July.

On 27 August, the 'Financial Gazette' reported that the government had abandoned its populist *indigenisation policy* "in a desperate attempt to lure offshore capital required to revive the country's disintegrating economy". The indigenisation law compelled foreign-owned companies to cede at least 51% of their shareholding in locally based companies to blacks or specific entities designated by government. However, it appeared there was a reversal in the reversal. In October, the combative new indigenisation minister, Patrick Zhuwao, announced that Zimbabwe would be imposing an additional tax burden on foreign-owned companies. The proposed 10% empowerment levy to fund indigenisation and economic empowerment would be raised to 12.5% in 2017. The change in policy appeared to reflect the factional struggles within ZANU-PF. Zhuwao was a leading member of the G40 faction while Finance Minister Chinamasa was believed to be in the Mnangagwa camp.

On 26 November, Finance Minister Chinamasa presented the *2016 national budget* with the theme "Building a Conducive Environment that Attracts Foreign Direct Investment". Chinamasa proposed a $ 4 bn budget. At $ 3.7 bn, recurrent expenditure was 92.1% of the budget. Revenue was projected at $ 3.9 bn in 2016. The $ 150 m deficit (1.1% of GDP) was to be funded by local borrowing. Chinamasa projected a GDP growth rate at market prices of 2.7% for 2016. Although expenditure on wages was expected to fall to 80% of the total budget, it would still increase by 2.7% in 2016.

Zimbabwe in 2016

Intraparty factionalism and succession struggles within the Zimbabwe African National Union-Patriotic Front (ZANU-PF) hogged the news throughout the year. There were rumours and speculations about opposition coalitions ahead of the 2018 elections. One of the major developments was the fallout between war veterans and President Mugabe. Speculation and gossip about Mugabe's health continued unabated. While foreign relations with the usual friends remained good, there was no sign of improvement in relations with Western countries and multilateral lenders. These strained relations were characterised by arguments about 'illegal' Western sanctions and human rights abuses. The economy showed no sign of improvement, with cash shortages worsening. This gave rise to another talking point for most of the year: the controversial introduction of so-called bond notes.

Domestic Politics

The ZANU-PF *succession struggles*, which had been obvious during the party's 15th Annual People's Conference in December 2015, escalated. With the Mujuru faction almost completely purged from the party, the main factions were Team Lacoste, reportedly aligned to Vice President Emmerson Mnangagwa, and Generation 40 (G40), widely seen as being aligned to President Robert Mugabe's wife, Grace Mugabe. In the run-up to an important ZANU-PF politburo meeting, on 2 February, the 'Daily News' quoted a ZANU-PF insider as saying Mugabe was "between a rock and a hard place" as both factions had some of his most trusted lieutenants among their ranks. On 30 January, Mugabe did not take sides. Instead, he pleaded for unity in the party, pointing out that "leaders are chosen at the [party] congress". Throughout the year, groups and senior party

 | DOI:10.1163/9789004404335_010

members within ZANU-PF became embroiled in the fractious succession politics. The Zimbabwe National Liberation War Veterans Association (ZNLWVA) threatened to bar Higher Education Minister Jonathan Moyo and Saviours Kasukuwere, the national political commissar – both of the G40 faction – from attending politburo meetings. On 8 February, the ZANU-PF Women's League secretary for finance, Sarah Mahoka, a known G40 member, challenged Mnangagwa to "come out clean" about his presidential ambitions. On 10 February, at a ZANU-PF rally attended by Robert Mugabe and the two vice presidents, Mahoka rebuked Mnangagwa, warning that he risked death if he did not rein in party officials abusing his name and campaigning for him to succeed the president. The fact that Mahoka was never rebuked by the party was taken as evidence that Grace Mugabe was behind the attack on Mnangagwa. *Mnangagwa's political career* was seemingly in danger after Grace Mugabe attacked him at a rally on 12 February. In the thinly veiled attack, she accused Mnangagwa of deception and working to topple her husband, among other things. There was speculation that the politburo meeting scheduled for 10 February would be the end of *Jonathan Moyo*, who was engaged in public Twitter wars with members of Team Lacoste. However, after the meeting the G40 faction seemed to have fared better than Team Lacoste. The political careers of key Mnangagwa allies were uncertain after they appeared before the party's National Disciplinary Committee on 16 February. The most prominent casualties were outspoken War Veterans Minister Christopher Mutsvangwa and his wife.

War veterans became actively involved in the divisive succession politics. The top leadership of the veterans, including Mutsvangwa, aligned themselves to Team Lacoste. On 18 February, anti-riot police disrupted a ZNLWVA meeting in Harare. They threw tear gas canisters into the crowd, which resulted in running battles. This signalled the breakdown of the relationship between President Mugabe and the veterans. In an unprecedented move on 22 July, the ZNLWVA appeared to have ditched Mugabe, issuing a strongly-worded statement that it would no longer support him in elections. The statement pointed out that the party leadership had "dismally failed" to deal with the economic problems besetting the nation. In an apparent attack on Mugabe, the group said it noted "with concern, shock and utter dismay the entrenchment of dictatorial tendencies, personified by the president and his cohorts which have slowly devoured the values of the liberation struggle". The ZNLWVA leadership. including its spokesman, Douglas Mahiya, and secretary-general, Victor Matemadanda, were arrested on charges of undermining the president's authority. Mugabe's relationship with the war veterans did not normalise for the rest of the year.

It had become the case that factional struggles were characterised by *expulsions and suspensions of senior party members.* On 18 March, ZANU-PF's Bulawayo province suspended 19 senior members for attending a war veterans meeting addressed by Mutsvangwa and Jabulani Sibanda, the former war veterans' leader who had been expelled from the party. Among those suspended was the former Matabeleland South governor, Senator Angeline Masuku. On 6 July, Mutsvangwa and his wife were expelled from ZANU-PF. He lost his parliamentary seat on 19 July. On 3 August, ZANU-PF expelled a further nine senior members, including the four top executives of the ZNLWVA, among them Mahiya and Matemadanda. When ZANU-PF held its 16th Annual People's Congress in Masvingo on 13–18 December, it was a divided party. Moyo's Twitter wars with members of Team Lacoste showed no signs of abating. In the end, the conference, on the theme 'Moving with Zim-Asset in Peace and Unity', was an unremarkable event with no major shifts in the factional struggles. The rumoured Women's League resolution to have a women's quota reinstated, allegedly to scuttle Mnangagwa' s presidential ambitions, did not materialise. The resolution would have meant that one of the vice presidents had to be a woman. Because Phelekelezela Mphoko, the other vice president was 'safe' by virtue of being from the former Zimbabwe African People's Union (ZAPU), the proposed clause was seen as targeting Mnangagwa. On 17 December, delegates confirmed Robert Mugabe as the sole *ZANU-PF presidential candidate* for the 2018 elections.

President Mugabe's health continued to be the source of speculation and rumours. It made headlines in April after a picture in the official press showed aides helping him as he was bending over to greet mourners at a funeral. Analysts said his aides were either holding his arms to prevent him from falling on top of mourners or supporting his failing hand. In August, Mugabe left a summit of southern African leaders apparently without warning and went to Dubai. This fuelled speculation that he had been taken seriously ill, with some rumours even suggesting he may have died. In November, Mugabe's health was again in the news when a video clip showed him walking painfully across the red carpet at the COP22 climate change summit in Marrakesh (Morocco).

The *fight against corruption* became tainted with succession politics when Higher Education Minister Moyo and his deputy were accused of corruption. In July, the Zimbabwe Anti-Corruption Commission (ZACC) revealed allegations of fraud and criminal abuse of duty, including that the two had siphoned off $ 400,000 from the Zimbabwe Manpower Development Fund. In October, Moyo admitted that he used the money to finance party projects and buy bicycles for traditional leaders in his constituency. There were reports that he was being protected from arrest in what was seen as an extension of ZANU-PF's factional wars. On 2 November, Moyo handed himself over to ZACC for questioning.

The Ministry of Finance and Economic Development announced in a circular distributed to MPs on 8 March that the government was planning to start *compensating white farmers* who had been evicted during the seizure of white-owned farms at the turn of the century. Compensation would be paid for land, improvements and equipment seized by the state. Commercial Farmers' Union (CFU) chief executive officer Hendrik Oliver doubted this, saying that most CFU members were sceptical of the offer because the government had not shown any commitment to compensating them since 2000. On 15 September, Minister of Finance and Economic Development Patrick Chinamasa revealed that the government had paid nearly

$ 43 m in compensation to white commercial farmers whose farms had been seized.

There was some major *industrial unrest* during the year. On 4 July, government workers went on strike over unpaid salaries. The government blamed this on the chronic cash shortage. Teachers, doctors and nurses were among the civil servants who stopped work because they had not been paid for more than a month. On 5 July, violent clashes between taxi drivers and police rocked Harare, leading to the arrest of 95 people. This coincided with the strike by doctors, teachers and nurses.

A resurgence among new *social movements* brought some life to protests, especially in urban areas. The most significant of these were #ThisFlag and #Tajamuka. The #ThisFlag movement was started in April through social media by the then little-known clergyman, *Pastor Evan Mawarire,* when he called for an end to the country's economic woes. By the second half of the year, the accidental movement had spread and become popular, especially among the youths in urban areas. On 6 July, #ThisFlag shut down Harare when it fronted a stay-away. Zimbabweans stayed at home and banks and most businesses closed operations because of the peaceful action. On 12 July, Pastor Mawarire was arrested after leading the campaign against alleged government corruption and the poor handling of the country's troubled economy. The police accused him of inciting public violence and disturbing the peace. There was an unprecedented demonstration of public support for Mawarire, with thousands of people reportedly attending his court hearing into the night of 13 July. On that day, the court freed him, ruling that the police had violated his rights. The magistrate told the packed courtroom that the decision to bring new charges against him was unconstitutional. The government apparently took Mawarire seriously, with President Mugabe himself speaking out against him on 19 July. He accused Mawarire of being foreign sponsored, calling for him to leave the country. Mawarire left the country, citing concerns about the security of his family. He ended up in the United States and stayed there for the rest of the year.

Human rights issues were mainly linked to alleged police brutality and curtailment of rights of assembly and movement. Mawarire was not the only person arrested for protesting. The most prominent cases of arrest, detention and brutality involved members of the protest group *Tajamuka-Sesijikile Campaign*. On 9 July, protest leader Promise Mkwananzi surrendered himself to police in Harare. They had been looking for him for participating in public unrest that had shut down Zimbabwe the previous week. He was facing charges related to alleged violence outside a supermarket said to be owned by Vice President Mphoko. A week after the protest, the police had reportedly arrested more than 200 people in connection with the shut down. There were reports of abductions and attempted abductions of protest leaders. On 6 July, two #Tajamuka activists, Lawrence Tembedza and Austin Nyakupinda, were allegedly abducted by suspected state security agents. Pastor Mawarire also alleged that suspected security agents had tried to abduct him but had failed.

Perhaps the most famous prisoner and symbol of the resistance and brutality was *Linda Masarira*, who was arrested on 6 July. She was detained for months in Chikurubi Maximum Security Prison, where she was reportedly locked up with dangerous male criminals. It was alleged by activists that the state was trying to make an example of her. Masarira was released on bail following a High Court judgement on 26 September. Another dogged protester who had run-ins with the state security apparatus was *Standrick Zvorwadza*, the chairman of the National Vendors Union of Zimbabwe. He was arrested at Rainbow Towers Hotel in Harare in June while protesting against Vice President Mphoko's continued stay in the hotel. He was charged with threats to commit malicious damage to property. On 18 August, Zvorwadza was admitted to hospital after heavily armed police attacked him while he was protesting at the Harare Central Police Station against alleged police ruthlessness in their treatment of vendors and prodemocracy activists.

It was a relatively quiet year in the opposition. Talks of an opposition grand coalition were perhaps the most dominant issue in *opposition politics*. On 28 April, Morgan Tsvangirai announced that the Movement for Democratic Change (MDC-T) national executive had mandated him to hold coalition negotiations with other opposition parties ahead of the 2018 elections. According to Eddie Cross, the party's secretary for local government, the MDC-T wanted any coalition to be built on two principles, "the interests of the country and the will of the people". Signalling that the talks would not be easy, Cross stated, "In the majority of cases we do not see this in our colleagues in the opposition movement." Despite pressures for an opposition coalition, there appeared to be discord on the issue within the MDC-T leadership, with some supporting it while others seemed unenthusiastic.

On 30 May, smaller opposition parties signed a coalition agreement in Harare. This marked the birth of the *Coalition of Democrats* (CODE), which was expected to field and support one candidate for president and more for other positions in elections from local government up to legislature level. The CODE signatories were the president of the Democratic Assembly for Restoration of the Economy, Gilbert Dzikiti, the president of the MDC-N, Welshman Ncube, the president of the Mavambo Khusile Dawn, Simba Makoni, the president of the Renewal Democrats, Elton Mangoma, and the president of Zimbabwe United for Democracy, Farai Mbire. Tendai Biti's People's Democratic Party and Dumiso Dambengwa's ZAPU were at the signing ceremony and gave solidarity messages, although they did not sign the agreement. MDC-T and Joice Mujuru's Zimbabwe People First did not attend. The MDC-T said they were not invited. Mujuru reportedly showed interest in the coalition but was waiting for the party's congress expected in August to give the green light to sign the agreement.

Opposition parties maintained their pressure for *electoral reforms* ahead of the 2018 elections. Operating under the National Electoral Reform Agenda (NERA) signed in December 2015, they staged several high-profile protest activities during the year. On 16 August, the

NERA signatories, among them the MDC-T, resolved to take Mugabe head-on in a protest march involving more than 200,000 opposition supporters. The NERA chairperson, former presidential affairs minister Didymus Mutasa, said the planned demonstration was aimed at forcing the Zimbabwe Electoral Commission to order the army, police and other units of the state security apparatus to stay out of partisan ZANU-PF politics. Police tried to block the demonstration and NERA had to go to court to be given the go-ahead. When the event finally took place on 26 August, law enforcement agents crushed it brutally. Police continued to ban and/or suppress NERA demonstrations for the rest of the year.

After a period of speculation about his health, on 27 June, MDC-T leader, *Morgan Tsvangirai* announced that he was undergoing treatment for colon cancer in South Africa. On 15 July, following a day-long meeting with his party's executive members, he announced the appointment of two new vice presidents for the MDC-T. The two new vice-presidents, Nelson Chamisa and Ellias Mudzuri, joined Thokozani Khupe, who had held the position for several years. The move was interpreted by some – particularly ZANU-PF sympathisers – as an indication that all was not well in the MDC-T.

There were a few *by-elections* during the year, which were all boycotted by the MDC-T. In October, independent candidate Temba Mliswa, who was backed by the MDC-T and war veterans, won the Norton by-election. In November, ZANU-PF won the Chimanimani West by-election by a margin of 8,000 votes. The parties that went up against ZANU-PF were the little-known Renewal of Democrats and the National Constitutional Assembly.

Foreign Affairs

The year saw no major shift in the country's foreign relations. As before, relations with most African and Asian countries and organisations were good. There was little change in relations with

OECD countries and major multilateral organisations. As expected, ZANU-PF and the government continued blaming Zimbabwe's economic woes on 'illegal' Western sanctions. On 28 January, Mugabe ended his one-year term as the *chair of the AU*. In his hour-long speech, he condemned the West's involvement in Africa's affairs. He also spoke against whites, former colonialists, Westerners, US President Barack Obama and the UN.

Zimbabwe continued to be an active and enthusiastic participant in *SADC* affairs but was not the centre of attention. Mugabe attended the 36th Heads of State and Government Summit in Mbabane (Swaziland) on 30–31 August. Zimbabwe was not on the agenda. Civil society groups had tried to force discussions on human rights abuses in Zimbabwe, citing police brutality against citizens expressing their right to demonstrate and issues regarding the use of social media to push for social justice, but they did not succeed.

While relations with most of Africa were good, relations with *Botswana* did not seem to improve. On 21 September, Reuters reported that Botswana's President Ian Khama had said Mugabe should step aside without delay and allow new leadership to emerge because Zimbabwe was dragging down the whole of southern Africa. At the end of September, Mugabe reportedly turned down an invitation by his Botswana counterpart to attend Botswana's celebrations for its 50th anniversary of Independence.

In August, Mugabe cancelled a scheduled state visit to *Ghana*, where he was to be given an award. There was confusion surrounding the cancellation and the event itself. Some reports suggested that he was angry that the hosts had also invited Morocco's King Mohammed VI. However, the Ghanaian government reportedly claimed that it had not invited Mugabe. There were also reports that Ghana's President John Mahama, who was expected to confer on Mugabe the Millennium Lifetime Achievement award, was not going to be in Accra.

Relations with *South Africa* remained friendly. On 31 October, the inaugural meeting of the South Africa–Zimbabwe Bi-National

Commission started in Harare. The two countries agreed to set up a Joint Trade and Investment Committee to oversee their economic cooperation. The official opening on 2 November was co-chaired by President Jacob Zuma and President Mugabe and the two leaders also witnessed the signing of an Air Service Agreement.

Zimbabwe maintained good relations with *China.* On 3 August, China pledged $ 46 m toward the construction of a new Zimbabwean parliament building. The pledge was described as a 'gift' to Zimbabwe. It was reported that Chinese officials believed that Zimbabwe's current parliament building was too small for its lawmakers to work effectively. During the year, China opened its markets to Zimbabwean farm products. It also expanded its investments in Zimbabwe's housing and agriculture sectors, and made loans to upgrade its medical equipment in inner-city hospitals.

Zimbabwe–Russia relations remained strong. On 13 November, a delegation of Russian companies led by the deputy head of the Africa Division of the Ministry of Industry and Trade of the Russian Federation, Pavel Volosov, was in Zimbabwe and had a meeting with the government and some local companies. The two countries agreed to set up a forum to facilitate and promote trade and investments. This was hailed as evidence that economic relations between Zimbabwe and Russia were poised for strong growth.

There was no major shift in relations with the *EU*. On 15 February, following an annual review, the European Council adopted a decision extending EU restrictive measures against Zimbabwe to 20 February 2017. The measures continued to apply to President Mugabe, his wife and Zimbabwe Defence Industries. Measures against "five high ranking members of the security apparatus" would remain suspended. Significantly, "78 persons and eight entities", against whom measures had been suspended, would be removed from the list. The arms embargo would remain in place. On 9 June, the EU signed an EPA giving six SADC nations unlimited access to the economic bloc. Zimbabwe was not included.

Relations with the *United Kingdom* did not change much. The UK's goal in Zimbabwe remained "to encourage a peaceful, democratic society where the rule of law and human rights are adhered to, laying the foundations for long term sustainable development". This meant inevitable clashes with Zimbabwe, whose brand of sovereignty interpreted such statements as interference and part of a regime-change agenda. On 6 April, it was reported that the UK had taken the unusual step of blocking Mugabe's nomination for the new Zimbabwe ambassador to the UK. The man at the centre of the unusual move was Ray Ndhlukula, then deputy chief secretary in the president's office. He was said to be one of the biggest beneficiaries of Zimbabwe's controversial land reform programme.

Relations with the *US* did not improve. On 1 March, President Barack Obama extended targeted sanctions for another year, saying Mugabe's regime continued to represent "an unusual and extraordinary threat to the foreign policy of the United States". On 3 October, the US announced the lifting of sanctions on nine individuals and several companies in Zimbabwe, but Mugabe himself remained on the list

Relations with *multilateral organisations* were mixed. On 9 May, the IMF announced the completion of the 2016 Article IV Consultation Mission to Zimbabwe and the Third and Final Review of the Staff-Monitored Program (SMP). The IMF noted that economic difficulties had deepened and recommended immediate action, but also noted that the authorities in Zimbabwe had met all quantitative targets and structural benchmarks under the SMP. On 19 October, Zimbabwe cleared its arrears with the IMF as part of efforts to settle its overdue financial obligations to the institution. Towards the end of the year, Zimbabwe was frantically scrambling to secure $ 600 m from the AfDB to clear its arrears, but this was not achieved. There were indications that the World Bank was considering giving Zimbabwe $ 300 m to settle part of its arrears to the multilateral lender. However, reports suggested that the plan was thwarted due to mounting local and international pressure against the country's ambitious arrears clearance strategy.

Socioeconomic Developments

There was no let-up in the country's economic challenges during the year. *Economic indicators* did not improve much and deflationary pressures continued. Reserve Bank of Zimbabwe (RBZ) figures showed that the December consumer price index for all items was 96.2%. The annual inflation was –1.6%, compared with –2.4% in 2015. According to Economist Intelligence Unit (EIU) estimates, real GDP growth was –0.4%, a drop from 0.5% in 2015. The EIU put the nominal GDP at $ 15.5 bn, up from $ 14.4 bn in 2015. The current account balance was –$ 2.1 bn, compared with –$3.1 bn in 2015. Total international reserves dropped to $ 394 m. According to the 2017 budget statement, as at 31 October 2016, Zimbabwe's public debt stood at $ 11.2 bn or 79% of GDP. Of this $ 7.5 bn (53% of GDP), was external debt. On 4 February, the RBZ governor, John Mangudya, announced in his Monetary Policy Statement a return to *partial exchange controls*. He claimed Zimbabwe was losing $ 2 bn a year in illicit outflows.

Zimbabwe performed poorly in a number of *world ranking tables*. In the World Bank's Doing Business 2016, it was ranked 161st, four places down from 2015. The World Economic Forum's Global Competitiveness Report 2015–16 ranked Zimbabwe 125th out of 140 countries. There was some improvement in the 2016 Human Development Report, with Zimbabwe indexed at 0.516 and ranked 154th, up one place from 2015.

The country faced several *humanitarian challenges*. On 21 January, the governor of the RBZ, announced that the government had secured $ 200 m from the African-Export-Import Bank (Afreximbank) in lines of credit for grain imports. In February, Mugabe declared a state of disaster in rural areas hit by a severe drought. More than a quarter of the population faced food shortages. According to the UN Office for the Coordination of Humanitarian Affairs, the humanitarian situation deteriorated dramatically across the country. Post-harvest assessments and the July Report of the Vulnerability Assessment Committee (ZimVAC) indicated that up to 4.1 m people in rural areas would be affected by food insecurity during the peak hunger period (January–March 2017). This amounted to 42% of the rural population. In August, 2.2 m people needed urgent food assistance. The ZimVAC highlighted levels of food insecurity between 50% and 79% in 20 districts. About 4.3 m people would need water and sanitation services between September 2016 and March 2017. The nutrition situation also deteriorated. Four districts were above WHO thresholds for 'serious' or 'critical' Global Acute Malnutrition rates, and a further 16 districts were classified as 'poor'.

Harare reported several cases of *typhoid fever*, sparking fears of a major outbreak. On 25 January, the Harare City health director, said that six cases of the disease had been confirmed in the previous five days in various suburbs. In December, typhoid fever was suspected to have claimed the life of a 13-year-old girl in Mbare, Harare's oldest suburb. There were fears that it could spread to other suburbs due to persistent rains. In October, health authorities issued a *cholera and typhoid outbreak alert* in the capital due to severe water shortages. Large parts of Harare were then restricted to running water on only two days a week, and residents in both urban and rural areas turned to potentially contaminated sources of water for everyday use.

On *demographic indicators*, according to estimates, the death rate stood at 9.87 deaths per 1,000 population. Due to the deteriorating economic situation, the flow of Zimbabweans into South Africa and Botswana in search of better economic opportunities persisted. UN estimates put the net migration rate at –2.97 migrants per 1,000 population. Life expectancy for the total population was 58 years. The infant mortality rate was estimated at 38.4 deaths per 1,000 live births. The literacy rate remained above 90%, making Zimbabwe the leader in Africa.

Zimbabwe had the fifth highest *HIV* prevalence in SSA. UNAIDS figures showed that 1.4 m people were living with HIV. The prevalence rate among adults aged 15–49 was estimated at 14.7%. Adults aged 15 and over living with HIV numbered some 1.3 m, plus 77,000 children aged 14 or under. Deaths due to AIDS were estimated at 29,000. There were 450,000 orphans under 18 due to AIDS.

As in 2015, the *education and health* delivery systems continued to experience problems of staffing, equipment and funding. Health and educational personnel continued to constitute a substantial part of the brain drain. Industrial action and threats of industrial action arising out of salary disputes were a constant feature throughout the year, further compromising these sectors. Delays in paying salaries and annual bonuses did not help boost morale. Throughout the year, Lazarus Dokora, the primary and secondary school minister, generated controversy with his zeal for an endless raft of reforms. In January, it was reported that the government was fine-tuning education policies. The minister said the changes would be implemented systematically and gradually. Among his proposed reforms were the teaching of all subjects in indigenous languages and the introduction of Islam and Buddhism to the curriculum.

On 12 April, Mugabe intervened to clarify the government's position on the controversial *indigenisation law* after a spate of public disagreements between Finance Minister Patrick Chinamasa and Indigenisation Minister Patrick Zhuwao over the implementation of the legislation in the financial services sector. Mugabe complained that the conflicting positions on how to implement the country's black empowerment legislation had caused confusion to potential investors and needed to be put to rest. In a statement released by Information Minister Christopher Mushowe, Mugabe subtly backed the finance minister's conciliatory tone. Chinamasa had announced that all foreign-owned financial institutions operating in the country had managed to submit credible indigenisation plans before the 31 March deadline. He said this after Zhuwao had threatened to shut down all companies that failed to submit "credible plans" by 1 April.

In May, the RBZ announced that it would issue *bond notes* to curb the flow of money out of the country. Like the bond coins that had been introduced in 2014, the bond notes would be backed by the $ 200 m Afreximbank Nostro Support facility, which was expected to cushion the high demand for foreign exchange. RBZ Governor John Mangundya did not give a date for the introduction of the notes. There was widespread suspicion, with critics and opponents claiming this was an attempt to reintroduce the Zimbabwe dollar through the backdoor and widespread scepticism that it would bring a return to the days of hyperinflation fuelled by the collapse of the Zimbabwe dollar. Mangudya rejected these criticisms and emphasised that the introduction of the notes was only a precaution against illicit financial flows. This triggered debate, protests and litigation – most prominently a law suit brought by the former vice president, Joice Mujuru. The controversy dragged on as the issuing of the bond notes was repeatedly delayed. On 18 November, the government finally gazetted the *Reserve Bank of Zimbabwe Amendment Bill 2016* to enable the central bank and the minister of finance and economic development to issue bond notes exchangeable at par value with the US dollar. The Act was deemed to have come into force on 31 October 2016 and the RBZ rolled out the controversial bond notes on 28 November. On the same day, a High Court judgement dismissed an application by a Harare businessman challenging the legality of Statutory Instrument 133 of 2016, which backed the release of bond notes into circulation.

In November, a survey by the Confederation of Zimbabwe Industries showed that local *manufacturing sector* capacity utilisation had increased by 18% to 47.4%. Experts pointed out that the increase was mainly the outcome of distortions resulting from the closure of hundreds of companies no longer considered in a nationwide survey.

In August, the government launched *Targeted Command Agriculture*. Some 2,000 farmers were expected to benefit from the agricultural scheme, which was aimed at ensuring food self-sufficiency.

The scheme was expected to target farmers near bodies of water, who could each put a minimum of 200 ha under maize cultivation. The mandate for each farmer was to produce at least 1,000 tonnes of maize. Each participating farmer was required to commit 5 tonnes per hectare towards repayment of government loans in the form of irrigation equipment, inputs and chemicals, mechanised equipment, electricity and water charges. Farmers would retain whatever they produced above the 1,000 tonnes. The programme would cost $ 500 m. Each farmer would receive $ 250,000.

On 8 December, the Finance and Economic Development Minister Patrick Chinamasa presented the *2017 national budget* with the theme 'Pushing Production Frontiers Across All Sectors of the Economy'. Chinamasa proposed a $ 4.1 bn budget. The economy was projected to grow by 1.7% in 2017. $ 2.9 bn in revenue was collected between January and October against a target of $ 3.2 bn, falling short by 9.8%. Cumulative expenditure for January to October amounted to $ 3.8 bn against a target of $ 3.3 bn, representing a $ 520 m overspend. Employment costs would account for 91% of revenue. Exports declined by 6.9% to $ 3.4 bn, against which the import bill stood at $ 5.4 bn.

Zimbabwe in 2017

The removal of President Robert Mugabe in what has been dubbed a 'soft coup' was the biggest story of the year. Before Mugabe's resignation, factional struggles in the Zimbabwe African National Union-Patriotic Front (ZANU-PF), in which his wife, Grace Mugabe, was the key player, dominated the news for most of the year. Away from ZANU-PF, the opposition remained divided and bickered constantly. While foreign relations with the usual friends remained good, there was very little improvement in relations with Western countries and multilateral lenders. Arguments about 'illegal' Western sanctions and human rights abuses persisted. Though some indicators improved, the economy showed no sign of significant improvement with cash shortages being one of the major challenges.

Domestic Politics

The year started quietly. The major developments in domestic politics related to justice. On 1 February, *#ThisFlag* activist and cleric Pastor Evan Mawarire was arrested by state security agents at Harare airport on his return from the US. He had spent six months outside the country. Mawarire was at the heart of the protests that had rocked Harare in 2016. He was charged with organising demonstrations and inciting violence. He was freed on bail by the High Court on 8 February. On the same day, the Constitutional Court dismissed a case against President Mugabe lodged by Promise Mkwananzi, a leading activist of the pressure group *#Tajamuka*. Mkwananzi had accused the ageing leader of violating the Constitution during the violently repressed protests in 2016. In the landmark case, Mkwananzi had asked the court to decide whether repressive actions by Mugabe had violated the Constitution.

 | DOI:10.1163/9789004404335_011

In May, the Pan-African research group *Afrobarometer* released the results of a survey that claimed 64% of Zimbabweans trusted President Mugabe and that 56% of Zimbabweans approved of the government's management of the country. The report also indicated that at least 36% distrusted opposition parties. The survey showed that 50% of adult Zimbabweans trusted the Zimbabwe Electoral Commission (ZEC). Opposition parties disputed the survey's results, which were given very wide coverage by the state-controlled media.

There was some activity in government's response to cybercrime but opposition parties claimed this was an attempt to clamp down on criticism. In May, it was reported that Zimbabwe was one of the countries hit by the WannaCry ransomware, a massive cyber-attack that hit computers in 104 countries. In the aftermath of the attack, on 17 May, Information and Communication Technology Minister Supa Mandiwanzira announced that the government would speed up the finalisation of the *Computer Crime and Cybercrime Bill.* Opposition parties expressed concern that the real intention behind the bill was to abuse the law to criminalise criticism of the president. This seemed to have been confirmed in August, when it was reported that the government was finalising the new cybercrime bill to criminalise false information posted on the Internet, revenge porn, cyber-bullying and online activity against the government, among other activities. Mandiwanzira said that the Cyber Crime and Cyber Security Bill would soon go to parliament, and was expected to be fast-tracked into law before the end of the year.

ZANU-PF *succession struggles* escalated. The main factions were 'Team Lacoste', aligned to Vice President Emmerson Mnangagwa, and 'Generation 40' ('G40'), aligned to Grace Mugabe. The factional struggles intensified during Presidential Youth Interface Rallies, which were organised by the ZANU-PF youth league ostensibly as occasions for Robert Mugabe to interact with the youth. The idea was to take the interface rallies to all ten provinces. The rallies started on 2 June with the Mashonaland East rally, which took place in Marondera. Commentators and Mnangagwa allies interpreted these rallies as being held to bolster the G40 faction as a strategy to advance Grace Mugabe's presidential ambitions. This appeared to be the case as the star of these rallies was undoubtedly Grace Mugabe. She used the rallies to attack Team Lacoste in general and Mnangagwa in particular. On 29 July, at the 5th Youth Interface Rally in Chinhoyi, Grace Mugabe launched a scathing attack on the Lacoste faction, accusing it of plotting against her husband and persecuting G40-aligned ministers. She singled out Higher and Tertiary Education Minister Jonathan Moyo, claiming that he had been falsely accused of corruption, although these charges continued to haunt him for most of the year.

Grace Mugabe's public statements on succession suggested that the factional struggles were heating up. On 27 July, *Grace Mugabe* challenged the president to name his preferred successor. This was the first time she appeared to contradict her husband. Though her stated reason for this naming was to end deepening divisions over the future leadership of the ruling ZANU-PF, it could also have been a sign that the succession battle was intensifying. She told a ZANU-PF rally that Mugabe had rejected her advice to name a successor, and hence her public challenge. This was a public contradiction of her own statement in February, when she stated that Mugabe should run 'as a corpse' in the 2018 election if he died before the vote. In an apparent reference to Mnangagwa, Mrs Mugabe warned associates of her husband from the period of the liberation struggle that they were also too old to take power. This was a rebuttal to those who were insisting that Mugabe should step down because his advanced age.

At the 6th Youth Interface Rally for Matabeleland South, held in Gwanda on 12 August, Vice President *Emmerson Mnangagwa* was rushed to hospital after falling ill. This incident exposed the rifts in ZANU-PF and worsened the relationship between Mugabe and his deputy. It later emerged that he had ingested poison. Official sources close to the vice president, however, downplayed social media claims that Mnangagwa had been poisoned. Rumours on social media linked his sudden illness to the ice-cream that had been served at the rally, and which was sourced from Mugabe's company, Gushungo Dairy Estate. On 14 August, Mnangagwa was airlifted to South Africa for medical attention after his health reportedly took a turn for the worse. Mnangagwa's illness fuelled suspicions that the poisoning was an assassination attempt. Mugabe and the G40 faction mounted spirited attempts to downplay the poisoning allegation. Grace Mugabe's outbursts and her angry public response to the rumours of food poisoning demonstrated how sensitive she was to the allegations, but her sensitivity and anger only fuelled the rumours of an assassination attempt on Mnangagwa. As the ZANU-PF succession wars reached a tipping point, Vice President Phelekezela Mphoko, then Acting President in the absence of Mugabe, and his counterpart Emmerson Mnangagwa openly traded accusations. On 30 September, Mnangagwa publicly told a memorial gathering that he had been poisoned. In a hard-hitting statement released on 3 October, Mphoko accused Mnangagwa of undermining Mugabe's authority and trying to destabilise the country by fanning ethnic tensions for political ends. In a rebuttal on 4 October, Mnangagwa said Mphoko had no authority to comment on his health issues and pointed out that Mphoko was "neither competent nor privileged to comment on my health because he is neither my doctor nor my employer".

President Mugabe showed the same sensitivity to the speculations about Mnangagwa's poisoning. On 1 September, at the 7th Presidential Youth Interface Rally in Gweru, he castigated some elements that he accused of peddling false allegations that Mnangagwa had fallen ill after eating ice cream from his dairy company. Mugabe claimed that Mnangagwa's South African-based doctor had briefed him on his deputy's ailment and ruled out food poisoning. On 5 October, Mnangagwa again said he had been hospitalised because he had been poisoned. This escalated the succession battles and was met with another angry outburst by Grace Mugabe, who insisted she had no reason to kill Mnangagwa because she was "the wife of the president". The relationship between Mugabe and his deputy never recovered. Grace Mugabe intensified her public attacks on Mnangagwa in the presidential interface rallies and at many events that she attended.

On 30 August, a *Grace Mugabe solidarity march* took place in Harare. The turnout was not as high as anticipated and Mnangagwa's Lacoste faction was blamed for sabotaging it. War veterans, who continued their criticism of Mrs Mugabe, and opposition parties poured scorn on the march. There was talk that Mugabe's wife was angling to be one of the vice presidents in place of Mnangagwa, which was seen as a path to the presidency. Suspicions of a *dynasty* in the making intensified when Mugabe's daughter, Bona Mugabe-Chikore, received two appointments in May in quick succession. On 24 May, she was appointed to the unpopular Censorship Board in a move that was interpreted as being intended to stifle criticism of President Mugabe. On 27 May, she was named as a board member of the new state-run Empower Bank.

In an explosive presentation to the *ZANU-PF politburo* on 19 June, Higher and Tertiary Education Minister Jonathan Moyo alleged that Mnangagwa and his Lacoste loyalists were aiming to succeed Mugabe through a number of schemes. On 4 October, Mnangagwa responded to the politburo, accusing Moyo of being a CIA agent working to destroy ZANU-PF from within. In a lengthy report, Mnangagwa claimed that Moyo was working with Western diplomats and officials against ZANU-PF. Mnangagwa reportedly accused Moyo and his G40 faction counterpart, Minister of Local Government, Rural Development and National Housing Saviour Kasukuwere, of secretly conniving to reduce Mugabe's powers by challenging ZANU-PF's 'one centre of power' principle and leaking confidential information to the press.

In what was interpreted as a reflection of the factional struggles in ZANU-PF, on 9 October, Mugabe announced a shock *cabinet reshuffle.* He dropped three ministers and reassigned ten others. Suspicions that this was an expansion of intra-party factionalism were given credence when Mugabe took the Ministry of Justice from Mnangagwa and gave it to Central Intelligence Organisation director-general Happyton Bonyongwe. Those axed from the cabinet included Priscah Mupfumira (Public Service), Tshinga Dube (War Veterans) and Abednico Ncube (Rural Development), all of whom were believed to be sympathetic to Mnangagwa. Patrick Chinamasa, a high profile Mnangagwa ally, was reassigned from the Finance and Economic Development Ministry to a new ministry, the Ministry of Cyber Security, Threat Detection and Mitigation. Zimbabweans jokingly referred to him as 'Minister of WhatsApp'. On 7 October, Mugabe had warned of the reshuffle, saying it was targeted at underperformers, but there was strong belief within ZANU-PF that Mugabe wanted to weaken Mnangagwa by getting rid of his allies.

In the last quarter of the year, the Presidential Interface Rallies continued and Grace Mugabe's *public attacks and humiliation of Mnangagwa* at the rallies intensified. The factional battles came to a head during the 9th Interface Rally in Bulawayo on 4 November. During her speech, Grace Mugabe was booed by what her allies claimed were people hired by Mnangagwa. She was visibly angry, and so was President Mugabe who, for the first time, publicly threatened to fire Mnangagwa the next day. In an indication of Mrs Mugabe's power, on 10 November, four people appeared in court on charges of undermining President Mugabe's authority after his wife was heckled at the Bulawayo rally. The Bulawayo rally was seen as marking the beginning of the end for Mnangagwa and Team Lacoste and the ascendency of Grace Mugabe to the presidency.

On 5 November, Grace Mugabe 'interfaced' with indigenous churches at Rufaro Stadium in Harare. In her speech, she launched her longest and most vitriolic attack on Mnangagwa. In her publicly broadcast speech, she gloated over her husband's threat to fire Mnangagwa, hinting that the end was near for the vice president. Obviously referring to Mnangagwa, Mrs Mugabe told the rally that "the snake must be hit on the head". On 6 November, *Mnangagwa was removed from his post* as vice president. Media, Information and

Broadcasting Services Minister Simon Khaya Moyo announced that Mnangagwa had displayed "traits of disloyalty" and that his "conduct in discharge of his duties" was "inconsistent with the responsibilities". Mnangagwa was also expelled from the ruling party. The sacking made it more likely that Grace Mugabe was on the way to being vice president and then president of Zimbabwe. On 6 November, the ZANU-PF youth league endorsed Grace Mugabe as the right candidate to occupy the vice presidency ahead of the extraordinary congress set for December. In what seemed to be a choreographed speech at the ZANU-PF politburo meeting on 8 November, the second vice president, Phelekezela Mphoko, urged President Mugabe to quickly appoint Mnangagwa's successor, saying that he was "now lonely". Mphoko said Mugabe should not be afraid or ashamed to appoint his wife as vice president, insisting that the people had "identified the one they want".

In what was to be the beginning of a fast-moving chain of events, in an unprecedented move on 13 November, *General Constantino Chiwenga*, the commander of the Zimbabwe Defence Forces warned that the military would not hesitate to step in to end purges against former liberation war fighters in ZANU-PF. This was a clear response to the sacking of Mnangagwa. Chiwenga, a political ally of Mnangagwa, said ZANU-PF had been hijacked by people who had not fought in the 1970s liberation war – a clear reference to the G40 faction and Grace Mugabe. Chiwenga reminded "those behind the current treacherous shenanigans that, when it comes to matters of protecting our revolution, the military will not hesitate to step in". His statement was read out at a news conference attended by the army top brass but the state-controlled press and public broadcaster ignored it. Responses were quick. On 14 November, a statement issued by the ZANU-PF youth league, and read by Secretary for Youth Kudzanayi Chipanga, condemned Chiwenga, telling him to first account for the $ 15 bn missing from the country's diamond sales, as he, together with Mnangagwa, presided over the country's diamond revenues. The youth league said they were ready to die for Mugabe.

Jonathan Moyo used Twitter to contemptuously dismiss Chiwenga's warning. On the same day, through its Secretary for Information Khaya Moyo, ZANU-PF called Chiwenga's statement "treasonous". Khaya Moyo said Chiwenga's utterances did not represent the rest of the command element and were meant to disturb national peace and stability, stating that "the gun seeks to overreach by dictating to politics and norms of constitutionality".

In the early hours of 15 November, army soldiers deployed in central Harare, taking control of state television, surrounding government ministries and sealing off Robert Mugabe's official and private residences. This was the beginning of what was later to be termed a *'soft coup'.* At 1:26 am, Major General Sibusiso Moyo appeared on state television and declared that the army was taking what he called "targeted action" against the "criminals" around Mugabe "who were committing crimes that are causing social and economic suffering ... in order to bring them to justice". The army spokesman insisted that this was not a takeover of the government but a move by the army "to pacify a degenerating political, social and economic situation" which, if not addressed, would cause violent conflict. Several government ministers linked to the G40 faction were reported to have been arrested. It later turned out that the G40 members arrested were Finance and Economic Development Minister Ignatius Chombo, and the combative ZANU-PF Secretary for Youth, Kudzanayi Chipanga. Mugabe and his wife were effectively under house arrest. Moyo, Kasukuwere and Patrick Zhuwao, the three most prominent members of Grace Mugabe's G40 faction skipped the country and Vice President Mphoko was also abroad.

Thousands of people celebrated the army takeover and urged Mugabe to step down. With police nowhere to be found, people could gather and march without police repression. They tore down pictures of Mugabe and marched to his office and residence. On 17 November, President Mugabe made his first public appearance since being confined to his house. He presided over the graduation at the Zimbabwe Open University as its chancellor. His wife was not with him and there were rumours that she had left the country, though these turned out to be false. *Negotiations*, mediated by Jesuit priest Fidelis Mukonori were reportedly going on behind the scenes to persuade Mugabe to step down. It was reported that he had insisted that he could not resign to legitimise a coup. On 16 November, Mugabe was pictured smiling as he took part in talks with an army general and South African government ministers at State House.

The 'soft coup' had widespread public backing, especially in Harare. The Zimbabwe National Liberation War Veterans Association called for a huge turnout in support of the military takeover. On 17 November, at least eight out of ten ZANU-PF provinces voted for Mugabe to resign as president and party secretary, for Grace Mugabe to be fired from the party and for Mnangagwa to be reinstated as a member of the Central Committee. Mnangagwa had by then left the country, reportedly fearing for his life, and was reported to be in South Africa. Groups opposed to Mugabe backed the military, with #ThisFlag leader Pastor Evan Mawarire urging people to turn up for the solidarity march planned for 18 November. On 19 November, Mugabe was expected to resign in a national address on live television but, when he did address the nation, he did not announce his resignation. Instead, in a rambling 30-minute address, he offered no concessions. There was speculation that he had swapped speeches. ZANU-PF warned it would seek to impeach him if he failed to resign by midday on 20 November. After the speech, the ZANU-PF chief whip announced that parliament would proceed with impeaching Mugabe on 21 November.

On 21 November, parliament heard charges in Mugabe's *impeachment proceedings*. MPs cheered as they listened to allegations against him, including that he had "allowed his wife to usurp constitutional power" and that he was "of advanced age". The impeachment motion was introduced by ZANU-PF and seconded by the opposition MDC and crowds gathered outside parliament in support of the proceedings. On 21 November, *Mugabe resigned*. In a letter read out by the speaker of parliament, he said the decision was voluntary and he had made it to allow a smooth transfer of power. The news halted the impeachment hearing. MPs and crowds celebrated and

ZANU-PF said former vice president Mnangagwa would succeed Mugabe. On 24 November, *Mnangagwa was sworn in as president* in a packed National Sports Stadium, having returned to Zimbabwe two days before.

On 30 November, the newly inaugurated President Mnangagwa named a *new cabinet* comprising new and old faces. Some of the old faces were Patrick Chinamasa (Finance and Economic Development), Obert Mpofu (Home Affairs) and Kembo Mohadi (Defence, Security and War Veterans). Among the new faces were key figures from the military. They included Major General Sibusiso Moyo (Foreign Affairs) and Air Marshal Perrance Shiri (Lands, Agriculture and Rural Resettlement). Opinion was divided on the new cabinet, with the opposition dismissing it as being made up of "dead wood". The *ZANU-PF extraordinary congress* was held on 15 December, trimmed down to one day of business on a reduced budget. On 18 December, Police Commissioner-General Augustine Chihuri, seen as a member of the G40 'cabal', was retired as the commissioner general of the Zimbabwe Republic Police. Deputy Commissioner Godwin Matanga was appointed as acting commissioner general. Like many Zimbabweans, the opposition cheered the firing of the unpopular Chihuri. On 23 December, Mnangagwa appointed now-retired army boss Constantino Chiwenga and Kembo Mohadi as vice presidents of ZANU-PF and, on 27 December, they were appointed as Zimbabwe's new vice presidents.

Foreign Affairs

Relations with most African and Asian countries and organisations remained good. There was little change in relations with OECD countries and major multilateral organisations. ZANU-PF and the government continued blaming Zimbabwe's economic woes on 'illegal' *Western sanctions.*

Zimbabwe continued to be an active and enthusiastic participant in *SADC* affairs but, unlike in previous years, was not the centre of attention. Mugabe attended the 37th Heads of State and Government Summit in Pretoria (South Africa) on 19–20 August. For the second year running, Zimbabwe was not on the agenda. Mugabe was not accompanied by his wife, whose absence was possibly due to her having been accused of assault (see below).

Relations with *South Africa* remained friendly, but they were tested. On 14 August, Gabriella Engels, a 20-year-old model, claimed *Grace Mugabe* had assaulted her with an extension cord at a Sandton Hotel in Johannesburg on 13 August and there was speculation that Grace Mugabe could face prosecution. Diplomatic immunity could only be granted if she had been in the country on official business, but reports were that this was a private health-related visit. On 16 August, it was reported that she was seeking diplomatic immunity. Acting National Police Commissioner Lesetja Mothiba stated that the position of the police was that she should go to court. Police Minister Fikile Mbalula said Grace Mugabe was due to appear in court but she did not attend, fuelling speculation she may have returned to Zimbabwe. South African police put border posts on red alert to prevent her fleeing. On 18 August, South Africa granted her diplomatic immunity, allowing her to avoid prosecution. The decision was widely condemned, but she returned to Zimbabwe on 19 August.

While relations with most of Africa were good, relations with *Botswana* continued to be frosty. On 3 October, Mugabe mocked Botswana's President Ian Khama for his unenthusiastic attitude towards campaigning for Botswana's Foreign Affairs and International Cooperation Minister Pelonomi Venson-Moitoi to become AU chairperson. Botswana said it would not respond to Mugabe's jibe due to his advanced age. On 7 November, Khama used social media to take another sly dig at Zimbabwe and Mugabe following the sacking of Mnangagwa, suggesting that Grace was responsible.

Zimbabwe maintained good relations with *China*. On 20 January, Chinese Ambassador Huang Ping commended the fruitful relations between the two countries and reiterated that his country had contributed to the economic growth of Zimbabwe, as evidenced by the number of successful projects that were underway. Huang mentioned the completion of the Victoria Falls International Airport refurbishment, the commencement of the construction of the Zimbabwe Parliament Building and the Kariba South Hydro Power Station Extension. After the removal of Mugabe, China's role in the 'soft coup' came under scrutiny. Less than two weeks before the events, the then army chief Constantino Chiwenga visited Beijing for a meeting with Chinese Defence Minister Chang Wanquan on 5 November. Amid speculation, China's Foreign Ministry insisted the meeting was a "normal military exchange as agreed by the two countries". There was speculation that Chiwenga was seeking China's support for a move against Mugabe. Whatever China's role in the coup, Beijing's priority was ensuring friendly bilateral relations that would allow commercial development in Zimbabwe to continue, regardless of who was in power.

Relations with *Russia* remained strong. On 29 May, Vice President Mphoko arrived in Russia for the 21st St Petersburg International Economic Forum, where Zimbabwe was expected to strengthen economic and investment ties with Russia. Mphoko was accompanied by a high-powered delegation comprising Industry and Commerce Minister Mike Bimha, Mines and Mining Development Minister Walter Chidhakwa and Finance and Economic Development Minister Patrick Chinamasa. Russia had shown keen interest in the country's industries and private sector investors were expected to visit the country to follow up on deals discussed on 3 June in St Petersburg.

There was no major shift in relations with the *EU*. On 24 February, following an annual review, the European Council adopted a decision extending EU restrictive measures against Zimbabwe. The measures continued to apply to President Mugabe, his wife and

Zimbabwe Defence Industries. The EU also introduced an exception to its arms embargo, allowing for the export of certain explosive substances solely for use in civilian mining and infrastructure projects. On 5 June, the EU extended a $ 2.6 m grant to Zimbabwe to help improve human rights protection. The grant marked the resumption of EU direct development assistance to Zimbabwe after the bloc imposed sanctions in 2002. The fund was intended to support the rule of law through justice sector reforms and increase access to justice for all. The grant came under the framework of the 11th EDF signed between Zimbabwe and the EU in 2015. In October, Zimbabwe's agricultural sector received a boost after the EU made over $ 7 m available towards funding the training of agricultural extension workers as part of efforts to improve sustainable farming.

Relations with the *United Kingdom* did not change much. On 6 October, President Mugabe claimed Britain was open to dialogue with his regime after a meeting with Conservative MP Sir Nicholas Soames in Harare. The meeting was criticised by the opposition. On 29 November, UK Foreign Secretary Boris Johnson said that Britain could take steps to stabilise Zimbabwe's currency system and extend a bridging loan to help it clear World Bank and AfDB arrears, but such support depended on "democratic progress".

Relations with the *US* did not improve. On 16 January, President Barack Obama extended for another year sanctions that were targeted at members of Mugabe's inner circle, the military top brass and associated companies accused of undermining democracy. The opposition welcomed the extension. The Zimbabwean government was optimistic that relations with the US would improve after Donald Trump became president but, by September, nothing had changed. In his address to the UN General Assembly on 21 September, Mugabe called Donald Trump a "giant gold Goliath" who threatened to make other countries "extinct". Mugabe urged Trump to "blow your trumpet" in a way that would promote peace and the self-determination of countries, and not their extinction.

Relations with *multilateral organisations* were mixed. In May, Zimbabwe secured a syndicated loan put together by the African Export-Import Bank (Afreximbank) that would enable it to clear $ 1.7 bn of arrears with the World Bank and the AfDB. On 7 July, the IMF released the annual Article IV consultation report on Zimbabwe. It noted that, while many of the country's underlying strengths remained, some of its industrial and agricultural base had been eroded. The dollarised economy faced difficulties of diminishing net capital flows and an acute cash shortage. The IMF noted that, with re-engagement with creditors delayed, access to external financing was limited. Zimbabwe was yet to reach a deal with the World Bank and other foreign lenders over clearing arrears and implementing reforms. In July, the AfDB launched three projects worth $ 26 m that had been approved by the Bank's Board of Directors. On 23 September, Afreximbank signed a memorandum of understanding with the Reserve Bank of Zimbabwe (RBZ) for a $ 600 m nostro stabilisation facility. In December, the RBZ exchange control division approved and registered the bank's $ 600 m loan facility from Afreximbank.

Socioeconomic Developments

There were no significant changes in the country's economic challenges. *Economic indicators* did not improve much and deflationary pressures continued. RBZ figures showed that the December consumer price index for all items was 99.5%. The annual inflation rate was 3.5%, compared with –0.9 in 2016. According to Economist Intelligence Unit (EIU) estimates, real GDP growth stood at 2.9%, a rise from 0.6%, in 2016. The EIU put the nominal GDP at $ 17.2 bn, up from $ 16.6 bn in 2016. The current account balance was –$ 1.47 bn, compared with –$ 1.28 bn in 2016. Total international reserves rose to $439 m from $407 m in 2016. According to the 2017 budget statement, Zimbabwe's public debt stood at $ 13.58 bn or 74.9% of GDP. Of this, $ 7.55 bn (41.6% of GDP) was external debt.

Zimbabwe's performance in several key *world rankings* did not change significantly. In the World Bank's Ease of Doing Business Report, the country was ranked 159th, four places up from 2016. The World Economic Forum's Global Competitiveness Report 2017–18 ranked Zimbabwe 124th out of 137 economies, compared with 126th the previous year. In the 2016 Human Development Report, Zimbabwe was indexed at 0.516 and ranked 154th.

The country faced several *humanitarian challenges*. There were multiple hazards, including drought, floods and outbreaks of cholera and typhoid. According to post-harvest assessments and the July report of the Vulnerability Assessment Committee (ZimVAC) 1.1 m people were projected to be 'food insecure' during the peak hunger period of January to March 2018. This was a decrease from 4.2 m people projected during the same period in 2017. There was a decrease in the global acute malnutrition prevalence from 4.4% in 2016 to 3.2% in 2017. Thirty-seven districts were affected by flooding caused by torrential rains during the period February to April. The government responded by declaring a state of disaster and launched a humanitarian appeal. The country also experienced the escalation of a protracted typhoid outbreak, which increased in severity during January to March. Harare later experienced a resurgence of typhoid and, between October and December, 2,032 typhoid cases were confirmed, though no deaths were reported. A total of six cholera cases including three deaths were reported.

On *demographic indicators*, according to estimates, the death rate stood at 10.2 per 1,000 people. Due to the deteriorating economic situation, the flow of Zimbabweans out of the country in search of better economic opportunities persisted. UN estimates put the net migration rate at 8.5 migrants per 1,000 people. Average life expectancy for the total population was 64 years. The infant mortality rate was estimated at 32.7 deaths per 1,000 live births. The literacy rate remained above 90%, making Zimbabwe the leader in Africa.

On *HIV* prevalence, UNAIDS figures showed that 1.3 m people were living with HIV. The prevalence rate among adults aged 15–49 was estimated at 13.5%. Adults aged 15 and over living with HIV numbered some 1.2 m. HIV incidence was 3.03%. Deaths due to AIDS were estimated at 30,000. The coverage of adults and children receiving antiretroviral therapy was 75%.

The *education and health* delivery systems continued to experience problems with staffing, equipment and funding. Health and education personnel continued to constitute a substantial part of the brain drain. Industrial action and threats of industrial action arising out of salary disputes were a constant feature throughout the year, further compromising these sectors, and delays in paying salaries and annual bonuses did not help boost morale. As in 2016, Primary and Secondary Education Minister Lazarus Dokora generated controversy with his zeal for an endless raft of reforms.

According to the Confederation of Zimbabwe Industries (CZI), the *manufacturing sector* recorded 5.5% growth in volume output compared with 2016, while the weighted average capacity utilisation fell from 47.4% to 45.1%. The level of capital investment in the sector grew. This helped explain the growth in capacity that was not being fully utilised. The CZI survey showed that there was increased demand for foreign currency, attributable to increased production output as more firms imported raw materials.

On 7 December, Finance and Economic Development Minister Patrick Chinamasa presented the *2018 national budget* with the theme 'Towards a New Economic Order'. Chinamasa proposed a $ 5.7 bn budget, with revenue projected at $ 5.1 bn. The economy was projected to grow by 3.7% in 2018. The budget deficit was expected to be $ 1.7 bn, much higher than the originally projected amount of $ 400 m. The 2018 budget deficit was projected at $ 675.8 m. Employment costs were $ 3.3 bn and capital expenditure was $ 1.2 bn, translating to 5.5% of GDP. The import bill was still relatively high, with imports estimated to rise to $ 6.8 bn, from $ 6.4 bn in 2016, despite a sharp drop in food imports.

Printed in the United States
by Baker & Taylor Publisher Services